PAT BROWN, MBA

RowingMoney101

Using Rowing to Teach the Basics of Money

ABRAM 47 BROWN

First published by AbramBrown47 2026

First edition

ISBN: 978-1-967737-58-1

This book was professionally typeset on Reedsy.
Find out more at reedsy.com

Contents

Foreword

Rowing teaches you something most people never learn.

Progress is quiet.

There is no scoreboard flashing every few seconds. No highlight reels. No crowd noise telling you how you are doing. Most of the work happens before sunrise, in cold air, on flat water, when only the people in the boat know whether the effort was good or wasted.

Money works the same way.

The outcomes everyone notices come much later. What matters happens early, repeatedly, and often without recognition. The discipline to show up, maintain rhythm, and trust the process determines everything long before results appear.

This book is built on that truth.

Rowing is not about pulling harder every stroke. It is about timing, balance, efficiency, and trust in the system. The best crews are not frantic. They are composed. They understand that forcing the boat slows it down. They know that one rower out of sync can cost more than a lack of raw strength.

Financial success follows the same rules.

Most people think money problems come from not earning enough or not knowing enough. In reality, most mistakes come from poor rhythm, impatience, and abandoning fundamentals under pressure. People sprint when they should settle. They chase speed when they should protect balance. They panic mid-race instead of trusting the plan.

Athletes understand this instinctively in sport. The challenge is translating it to life after competition.

When the boat is docked and the structured schedule disappears, many athletes struggle. Not because they lost discipline, but because the environment that enforced it is gone. What used to be mandatory becomes optional. What used to be coached becomes self-directed. Without a new system, even the most disciplined competitors drift.

This book exists to replace that structure.

Rowing Money 101 is not about shortcuts, hot tips, or winning overnight. It is about building a financial approach that mirrors what great rowers already know. Establish the catch. Stay balanced. Hold a steady rate. Make clean adjustments. Finish strong.

You do not win long races by sprinting the first 500 meters. You win by staying composed when the race gets uncomfortable. You win by trusting that small, repeated efforts compound. You win by keeping the boat set when conditions change.

Money is a long race.

There will be rough water. Headwinds. Unexpected setbacks. There will be moments when pulling harder feels tempting and moments when quitting feels easier. This book does not pretend those moments disappear. It shows you how to navigate them without flipping the boat.

You will not find complicated formulas here. You will not find academic jargon. You will find fundamentals explained in a language athletes understand. Preparation. Reps. Discipline. Recovery. Adjustments. Trust.

The lessons in this book apply whether you rowed competitively or simply understand what it means to commit to a demanding sport. They apply whether your income arrives steadily or in waves. They apply whether you are early in your career or rebuilding after a transition.

Money, like rowing, rewards consistency more than intensity. It rewards patience more than ego. It rewards systems over motivation.

The best crews do not argue with the water. They adapt. They stay in sync. They focus on what they can control. They finish races knowing they respected the process, regardless of conditions.

That mindset is transferable.

If you approach your finances the way you approached training, you already have an advantage. If you apply the same discipline you showed in the boat, you can build stability, flexibility, and confidence over time. Not by pulling harder, but by rowing smarter.

This book is not here to impress you.

It is here to steady you.

To give you a rhythm you can trust when noise increases.

To help you stay upright when pressure builds.

To remind you that progress does not need applause to be real.

The long race is not about speed alone.

It is about control, endurance, and execution.

Set the boat.

Find your rhythm.

Stay in sync.

The finish line will take care of itself.

Introduction

Rowing teaches patience early.

Before there is speed, there is setup. Before power, there is balance. Before races, there are countless steady rows where nothing dramatic happens and nothing external confirms progress. You learn quickly that pulling harder does not automatically make the boat faster. In fact, forcing it often slows everything down.

Money works the same way.

Most people approach money like a sprint. Earn fast. Spend freely. Chase quick wins. Panic when conditions change. Then they are surprised when exhaustion sets in and progress stalls. Rowers understand something different. There is no finish line without the long row. You do not skip the middle and still arrive strong.

This book is about learning to row money the right way.

Why Athletes Struggle With Money After Competition

Athletes are not bad with money because they lack discipline. They struggle because the structure that once enforced discipline disappears.

In rowing, everything is scheduled. Training times. Erg sessions. On-water practices. Recovery. Nutrition. You do not decide whether to train. You decide how well you show up. After competition ends, that system vanishes. Financial decisions replace practice plans, but there is no coach calling lineups or setting the rate.

Without a new structure, even disciplined athletes drift.

Saving feels optional.

Planning feels distant.

Investing feels intimidating.

Mistakes do not show up immediately.

Money gives delayed feedback. That delay creates false confidence early and regret later. Rowers understand delayed feedback better than most. You can have a great stroke and not see speed until the crew settles. You can have poor rhythm and not feel the cost until the final meters.

The same dynamic applies financially.

There Is No Straight Line, Only a Long Course

Rowing races are rarely clean.

There is chop.

There are headwinds.

There are steering adjustments.

There are moments when the boat feels heavy for no obvious reason.

You do not quit because conditions are imperfect. You adapt. You keep the rate. You trust the process. Money follows the same pattern. Careers stall. Markets drop. Life intervenes. The people who succeed are not the ones who avoid rough water. They are the ones who stay upright through it.

This book does not promise smooth conditions.

It teaches balance.

Rhythm Matters More Than Raw Strength

In rowing, power without rhythm is wasted. Eight strong athletes out of sync lose to a disciplined crew working together. The boat rewards efficiency, timing, and repeatable effort.

Financial success is built the same way.

It is not about making the most money.

It is about keeping the most progress.

It is about steady habits repeated over time.

Budgeting is rhythm.

Saving is rhythm.

Investing is rhythm.

Rebalancing is rhythm.

You do not need perfect technique to move forward. You need consistency and awareness. Small improvements, applied daily, create momentum that compounds quietly.

This Is Not a Sprint Book

This is not a book about beating the market.

It is not a book about shortcuts.

It is not a book about forcing results.

It is a book about endurance.

Rowers know that the hardest part of the race is not the start. It is the middle, when fatigue sets in and no one is watching. Financially, that middle is most of life. This book is built for that stretch.

You will learn how to:

- Establish a clean catch with your finances
- Stay balanced when risk increases
- Hold rate when emotions rise
- Make adjustments without losing rhythm
- Finish strong without burning out

A Playbook for the Long Race

Rowing Money 101 is designed to feel familiar.

It uses the language of training, reps, film, adjustments, and seasons because athletes understand those concepts deeply. You already know how to commit to something difficult. You already know how to trust a process before results appear. You already know how to endure.

This book helps you apply those skills to money.

Not perfectly.

Not instantly.

But deliberately.

There is no finish line without the long row.

If you approach your finances the way you approached training, you will build stability before stress, confidence before panic, and options before urgency. You will stop reacting and start rowing with intention.

Set the boat.

Find the rhythm.

Respect the distance.

The long row is where real progress is made.

About This Book

Rowing is an honest sport.

There is nowhere to hide in the boat. If timing is off, everyone feels it. If balance is lost, progress slows immediately. If one rower pulls harder instead of rowing better, the shell suffers. Speed comes from rhythm, not force.

Money works the same way.

Most financial advice ignores this truth. It focuses on effort instead of efficiency. Earn more. Hustle harder. Take bigger risks. Push for faster results. That mindset produces short bursts of progress followed by long stretches of frustration.

Rowers know better.

You cannot muscle your way through a long race. You win by staying set, holding rate, and trusting small advantages repeated over time. This book uses rowing because rowing already teaches the skills money demands.

Why Rowing Is the Right Lens for Money

Rowing is not about dominance.

It is about discipline.

There are no shortcuts. No miracle strokes. No individual heroics that override fundamentals. Boats move when crews work together, apply power at the right time, and recover cleanly.

Financial progress follows the same rules.

Money rewards:

- Timing over intensity

- Consistency over bursts
- Systems over motivation
- Patience over ego

Rowing teaches you to respect distance. You learn quickly that the race is not decided in the first few strokes. Early mistakes compound. Late discipline matters. The middle of the race is where outcomes are shaped.

Most financial mistakes happen in the middle.

Not at the start.

Not at the end.

In the long, quiet stretch where attention fades.

This book exists for that stretch.

The Core Rowing Lessons Applied to Money

Every part of rowing maps naturally to financial decision-making.

The catch matters.

A poor catch costs energy and speed immediately. Financially, bad foundations do the same. No savings, unmanaged debt, and no plan create drag that compounds quietly.

Balance matters.

Rowing off balance wastes power. Financially, imbalance shows up as too much risk, too much spending, or too much cash sitting idle. Balance allows steady progress even in rough water.

Rate matters.

Rowing too fast early burns you out. Financially, chasing quick wins leads to mistakes. A sustainable pace keeps you moving without panic.

Recovery matters.

Rowers know recovery is not rest. It is preparation for the next stroke. Financially, recovery looks like planning, reviewing, and adjusting before problems grow.

Mid-race adjustments matter.

Great crews adjust without losing rhythm. Financially, rebalancing and course correction keep progress steady without emotional overreaction.

What This Book Is Not

This is not a book about beating the market.

It is not a book about extreme frugality.

It is not a book about turning money into identity.

It is not written for people looking for excitement.

It is written for people who understand endurance.

Rowing Money 101 does not promise speed. It promises stability. It does not offer hacks. It offers habits. It does not rely on motivation. It builds systems.

The goal is not to feel smart.

The goal is to stay upright.

Who This Book Is For

This book is for athletes who understand:

- Showing up matters more than showing off
- Reps matter more than intensity
- Progress is rarely dramatic
- Discipline outlasts motivation

You do not need to have rowed competitively to benefit. You only need to understand training, pressure, patience, and long-term effort. If you have ever committed to something difficult without immediate rewards, this book is written in your language.

Why the Long Race Wins

Money is not a sprint.

It is not even a single race.

It is a season made of thousands of strokes.

Some strokes feel powerful.

Some feel awkward.

Some feel wasted.

What matters is staying in sync with your plan long enough for compounding to work. That is where rowing provides clarity. You learn that effort without rhythm is wasted and that discipline without panic wins over time.

This book teaches you how to:

- Build a clean financial catch
- Hold balance under pressure
- Maintain a sustainable rate
- Adjust without losing composure
- Finish strong without burning out

Rowing teaches you to respect the process.

Money demands the same respect.

That is why rowing is the lens.

That is why this book exists.

Set the boat.

Trust the rhythm.

Row the long race.

Foolish Assumptions

Every good coach starts with assumptions.

Not excuses.

Not shortcuts.

Assumptions about effort, mindset, and accountability.

This book does the same.

Before getting into money mechanics, investing concepts, or long-term planning, it is important to be clear about what this book assumes about you. Not because everyone fits perfectly into these assumptions, but because the framework only works if you recognize yourself in them.

If these assumptions do not feel true yet, that does not disqualify you. It simply means this book is also about becoming this person again, just in a different arena.

Assumption One: You Understand Discipline Better Than Most People

This book assumes you know what discipline actually looks like.

Not motivation.

Not inspiration.

Not hype.

Discipline is showing up when you do not feel like it. It is following a plan even when progress is slow. It is repeating boring fundamentals long after the excitement wears off.

Rowers understand this deeply. Early mornings. Long steady rows. Erg pieces that test patience more than strength. You already know that results come from consistent effort, not from occasional intensity.

This book assumes you are capable of that level of discipline with money, even if you have not applied it there yet.

Assumption Two: You Respect Process More Than Shortcuts

This book assumes you do not believe in shortcuts.

You may enjoy speed when it is earned, but you know forced speed breaks systems. In rowing, you cannot cheat the catch. You cannot rush the slide without paying for it later. The boat always tells the truth.

Money works the same way.

If you are looking for hacks, tricks, or guaranteed outcomes, this book will frustrate you. It is built around process. Around rhythm. Around letting time do the heavy lifting.

This book assumes you are willing to commit to a process even when nobody is watching.

Assumption Three: You Can Handle Honest Feedback

Athletes are coached hard.

Mistakes are pointed out. Weaknesses are addressed directly. Progress requires honesty. This book assumes you can handle that tone.

There will be moments where the mirror is uncomfortable. Where habits are challenged. Where assumptions about money, spending, or risk are questioned.

That is not judgment.

That is coaching.

If something here feels confrontational, it is likely touching a blind spot. That is usually where growth starts.

Assumption Four: You Understand That Comfort Is the Enemy of Progress

Rowing is uncomfortable by design.

Growth happens in discomfort. Staying set in rough water. Holding rate when fatigue sets in. Trusting the stroke when quitting feels easier.

This book assumes you understand that comfort is not the goal. Stability is. Sustainability is. Control is.

Financial mistakes often come from chasing comfort. Spending to relieve stress. Avoiding planning because it feels overwhelming. Delaying decisions because the payoff feels far away.

This book assumes you are willing to be uncomfortable now to protect yourself later.

Assumption Five: You Are Willing to Think Long-Term

Rowers think in seasons, not moments.

You know that one bad practice does not define a year and one great race does not erase poor preparation. This book assumes you can zoom out and think in years, not weeks.

Money requires that perspective.

Small decisions repeated over time matter more than any single move. This book assumes you are capable of patience, even if the world around you rewards speed.

Assumption Six: You Are More Than an Athlete, But Sports Shaped You

This book does not assume your identity is only athletic.

It does assume that sports shaped how you think, compete, and respond to pressure. The discipline, resilience, and teamwork you learned did not disappear when competition ended. They just need a new outlet.

This book assumes you are willing to transfer those skills forward instead of trying to relive the past.

If These Assumptions Feel Uncomfortable

Good.

That usually means you care.

This book is not written for people who want to be entertained. It is written for people who want to be steady, capable, and prepared over the long race of life.

You do not need to be perfect.

You do need to be honest.

You do need to show up.

Rowing taught you how to do that.

This book assumes you are still that person.

How This Playbook Is Organized

Rowing rewards structure.

You do not show up to the boathouse and just pull. Sessions have a purpose. Warm-ups lead to drills. Drills lead to pieces. Pieces lead to recovery. Each part builds on the last. Skip steps and the boat never feels right.

This book is organized the same way.

Rowing Money 101 is not meant to be read like a novel or skimmed for highlights. It is a playbook. A training plan. A long-term program designed to build financial strength the same way rowing builds physical and mental strength.

Each part of the book mirrors a phase of rowing development and a phase of financial development. The order matters.

Part I: Catch and Fundamentals (Building the Base)

Everything starts with the catch.

In rowing, a poor catch ruins the entire stroke. You can be strong, fit, and motivated, but if the blade enters the water wrong, power is wasted. The same is true financially.

This section focuses on fundamentals:

- Understanding where your money actually goes
- Establishing saving and budgeting rhythm
- Learning how credit, debt, and banking really work

Nothing here is flashy. That is intentional. Just like early technical work in rowing, these chapters are about building a base that supports everything else. If this section feels slow, that is a sign it is doing its job.

Part II: Balance, Protection, and Staying Upright

Once the boat is moving, balance matters.

You do not row well if you are constantly worried about flipping. Financially, protection serves the same purpose. Insurance, risk awareness, and basic safeguards keep one mistake from ending the race.

This section focuses on:

- Understanding risk
- Protecting income and assets
- Avoiding common mistakes that capsize progress

Rowers know that staying upright is not passive. It takes awareness and adjustment. This part of the book builds that awareness financially.

Part III: Building Speed (Investing Fundamentals)

Speed comes from efficiency, not panic.

Once fundamentals and balance are established, you can start focusing on growth. Investing is where many athletes rush ahead without understanding mechanics. This section slows that impulse down.

You will learn:

- How markets actually work
- What owning stocks and bonds really means
- Why compounding rewards patience
- How diversification works without complexity

This is not about sprinting. It is about sustainable speed. The goal is to help you invest with confidence instead of emotion.

Part IV: Mid-Race Adjustments (Managing the Portfolio)

Great crews adjust without losing rhythm.

No race goes exactly as planned. Conditions change. Fatigue sets in. Smart crews make corrections early and calmly. Financially, this section teaches you how to manage what you have built.

You will learn:

- How to balance assets over time
- When to buy, hold, and ignore noise
- How and when to rebalance
- How to manage the mental side of money

This part of the book emphasizes discipline over reaction. Adjustments are part of the race, not a sign of failure.

Part V: The Long Pull and Life After Competition

The longest stretch is where most races are won.

This section focuses on real-life decisions that shape outcomes over decades:

- Taxes
- Retirement planning
- Housing and major purchases
- Career strategy
- Estate planning
- Family conversations about money

These chapters recognize that money decisions do not happen in isolation. They happen alongside careers, families, health, and aging. This is where rowing's endurance mindset matters most.

Part VI: Crossing the Line Strong

Finishing strong is intentional.

The final section brings everything together. It focuses on building the right support system, avoiding scams, and committing to long-term discipline. No heroics. No shortcuts. Just smart execution through the finish.

How to Use This Book

You can read this book straight through.

You can revisit sections as life changes.

You can treat chapters like training sessions and return to them when needed.

What matters most is not speed.

It is consistency.

If you respect the order, trust the process, and apply the lessons gradually, this playbook will do what it is designed to do. It will help you build rhythm, discipline, and confidence over the long race.

Set the boat.

Follow the structure.

Row one stroke at a time.

About Pat Brown

Pat Brown understands structure, discipline, and long preparation cycles because he lived them long before working in finance.

Pat played college football at the University of Kansas from 1994 to 1999 and was named team captain for the 1999 season. Years in the locker room shaped how he thinks about accountability, preparation, leadership, and effort. Those lessons did not end when football ended. They became the foundation for how he approaches money, decision-making, and long-term planning.

After his playing career, Pat transitioned into financial services and built a career as a financial advisor and wealth manager. He works with individuals, families, business owners, and athletes navigating increasingly complex financial lives. Over time, he noticed something familiar. Most financial challenges are not caused by a lack of intelligence. They are caused by poor structure, rushed decisions, emotional reactions, and the absence of a long-term plan. Those problems mirror what happens in sports when rhythm breaks down.

Pat pursued advanced education and professional development to deepen his work. He earned an MBA along with industry designations including ChFC®, RICP®, and CAP®. His background blends formal education with real-world experience across financial planning, retirement income strategies, tax planning, risk management, and philanthropy. He operates where theory meets pressure, which is the same place athletes are trained to perform.

As college sports evolved with the introduction of Name, Image, and Likeness opportunities, Pat saw a growing education gap. Student-athletes were gaining access to income, contracts, and endorsements without the financial knowledge needed to manage cash flow, taxes, business structures, and long-term consequences. Opportunity was arriving before preparation. For anyone who has trained for competition, that imbalance was obvious and concerning.

That reality became the catalyst for Pat's work in the NIL space.

He began focusing on financial education designed specifically for athletes and their families. Clear language. Real scenarios. No jargon. No lectures. The same way a coach teaches technique, Pat teaches money concepts through structure, repetition, and practical application. His work grew as families, schools, and organizations recognized the need for athlete-centered financial education.

Pat has since become a recognized voice in athlete financial literacy and NIL planning. He has been interviewed by national publications and platforms including Financial Planning, Yahoo, and ESPN Andscape, where he shares insights on NIL planning, financial education gaps, and the challenges student-athletes face as income arrives earlier in life.

These experiences led Pat to author a series of practical, athlete-focused books designed to function like playbooks rather than textbooks. His NIL-related titles include Financial Literacy for NIL, Financial Literacy for NIL for Parents of Student Athletes, Financial Literacy for NIL for High School Students, and Financial Literacy for NIL for International Student Athletes. Each book is written to be accessible, direct, and grounded in real decisions athletes encounter, not abstract theory.

Pat also created a growing collection of sport-specific financial education books. These titles include Football Money 101, Baseball Money 101, Basketball Money 101, Cheer Money 101, Dance Money 101, Gymnastics Money 101, Hockey Money 101, Lacrosse Money 101, Rowing Money 101, Soccer Money 101, Softball Money 101, Tennis Money 101, Track Money 101, Volleyball Money 101, and Wrestling Money 101. Each book translates the culture, discipline, and mindset of a specific sport into financial lessons athletes can apply long after competition ends.

Rowing Money 101 fits naturally into that mission.

Rowing teaches patience, rhythm, balance, and respect for the long race. Those lessons mirror how money actually works. Progress is quiet. Efficiency matters more than force. Small mistakes compound. Consistency beats intensity. Pat uses rowing because it reflects how financial success is built in real life, one disciplined stroke at a time.

To extend this work beyond books, Pat founded Former Student Athlete, a platform created to support athletes navigating life after sports. Former Student Athlete focuses on education, community, and real-world resources related to financial literacy, career transitions, health, identity, and long-term success once the uniform comes off. This work can be explored at www.formerstudentathlete.com, www.financialliteracyfornil.com, and www.financialliteracyforstudentathletes.com.

Pat is easy to find through a Google search, on LinkedIn, or on Twitter, where he regularly shares insights on athletes, money, and life after sports.

Pat's work is rooted in a belief shaped by both competition and finance.

Athletes deserve a better playbook for life after sports.

And financial education should arrive before opportunity turns into regret.

Part I: Catch and Fundamentals (Building the Base)

Everything starts with a clean catch.

Every rower learns this early.

You can be strong. You can be fit. You can want it badly. None of that matters if the catch is sloppy. A late blade. A rushed slide. Poor connection at the front end. The boat feels heavy, unstable, and slow no matter how hard you pull.

Good rowing does not start with power.

It starts with position, timing, and connection.

Money works the same way.

Before growth, before investing, before strategy, there has to be a clean financial catch. That means understanding the basics, setting your position correctly, and creating solid connection with your money. Without that foundation, everything that follows feels harder than it needs to be.

This section of the book is about building that base.

Why Fundamentals Matter More Than Force

Rowers know you cannot muscle bad technique into good speed.

The harder you pull with a bad catch, the worse the boat feels. Fatigue sets in faster. Frustration builds. Eventually, people start blaming conditions instead of mechanics.

Financially, the same thing happens.

People try to invest before understanding cash flow.

They chase returns without emergency reserves.

They focus on earning more without controlling spending.

They pull harder instead of rowing cleaner.

The result is unnecessary stress and stalled progress.

Fundamentals are not exciting, but they are decisive. They determine whether effort turns into forward movement or wasted energy.

What a "Clean Catch" Means With Money

In rowing, a clean catch means the blade enters the water smoothly, fully connected, and on time. The stroke feels light and controlled. Power transfers efficiently through the system.

Financially, a clean catch means:

- You know where your money goes
- You spend intentionally, not accidentally
- You save automatically, not emotionally
- You understand basic tools like banking, credit, and debt

It does not mean perfection.

It means awareness and alignment.

A clean catch allows everything else to work.

Building the Base Before Adding Pressure

Rowing programs do not start seasons with race pieces.

They start with steady state.

They start with drills.

They start with technique.

Not because racing is unimportant, but because racing without a base leads to breakdown.

This section of the book does the same thing.

You will not find shortcuts here.

You will not find hype.

You will not find pressure to perform.

You will find:

- How to understand your financial snapshot
- How to build saving rhythm
- How to manage credit and debt without drag
- How to use banking tools correctly

These are the steady meters that prepare you for everything else.

Why Athletes Often Skip This Part

Athletes are wired for competition.

They want progress.

They want results.

They want to know if they are winning.

Fundamentals feel slow.

They feel repetitive.

They feel beneath someone who has already proven discipline.

That mindset is dangerous.

The strongest rowers respect fundamentals the most because they know breakdowns start there. Financial mistakes rarely come from lack of effort. They come from ignoring basics until problems surface later.

Skipping this section is like skipping technique work and hoping fitness saves you.

It will not.

Rhythm Is Built Here

Rhythm is not something you turn on during a race.

It is built during boring meters.

Financial rhythm is the same.

Budgeting is rhythm.

Saving is rhythm.

Paying yourself first is rhythm.

Avoiding panic is rhythm.

This section helps you establish a cadence you can maintain when pressure increases. When income fluctuates. When expenses rise. When distractions show up.

If rhythm exists, you adjust.

If rhythm does not exist, you panic.

What This Section Prepares You For

Everything that follows depends on this foundation.

Investing only works if cash flow is stable.

Risk only makes sense if protection exists.

Growth only compounds if behavior is consistent.

Part I is not about moving fast.

It is about getting set.

Once the boat is balanced and connected, power becomes effective. Without that, every stroke costs more than it should.

A Coach's Perspective

A coach would not sugarcoat this.

Get the catch right.

Do not rush the process.

Details matter.

You cannot cheat fundamentals.

Earn the right to move on.

This section earns that right.

How to Use Part I

Read it slowly.

Apply it deliberately.

Revisit it when things feel off.

If later chapters feel stressful or confusing, the answer is often back here. Something at the front end needs attention.

That is not failure.

That is rowing.

Set the blade.

Feel the connection.

Build the base.

Everything starts with a clean catch.

Chapter 1: Why Money Feels Confusing After the Boat Is Docked

The first time the boat is docked for good feels strange.

For years, your schedule revolved around training blocks, seat races, erg tests, and regattas. You knew when to show up, how hard to push, and what progress looked like. Even when rowing was brutal, it was clear. The system existed. The expectations were defined.

Then it ends.

No more lineup cards. No coach setting the rate. No training plan taped to the boathouse wall. You are still the same disciplined person, but the structure that organized your effort disappears. Money quietly takes the place of training, but no one ever taught you how to row it.

That is why money feels confusing after the boat is docked.

Not because you are bad with it.

Not because you are undisciplined.

Because the system was never built.

Why Financial Literacy Is Rarely Taught to Athletes

Athletes grow up in performance environments.

Your job was to train, compete, recover, and repeat. Financial education was never part of the program because it was not considered urgent. Coaches focused on speed. Schools focused on eligibility. Families assumed money would "work itself out later."

That later arrives faster than expected.

Rowers understand specialization. You trained for performance, not for accounting. No one would expect you to learn rigging theory during race week. Money was treated the same way. Something important, but always postponed.

The problem is that money decisions start long before people think they should. First paychecks. Travel costs. Equipment. Housing. Credit cards. Small decisions quietly stack without guidance.

In rowing terms, this is being sent out on the water without learning how to set the boat. You can still row, but everything feels unstable.

Money Myths Passed Down in Boathouses

When education is missing, myths fill the gap.

Athletes pass advice the same way they pass rumors. Through teammates, older rowers, family members, and social circles. Some of it is well-meaning. Much of it is wrong.

A few common ones show up repeatedly.

"Just work harder and it will fix itself."

That mindset works in training. It fails financially. Money does not reward effort alone. It rewards structure and consistency.

"You'll figure it out when you make more."

Income helps, but it does not replace fundamentals. Many people earn more and feel more stressed because spending grows faster than structure.

"Investing is risky. Saving is safe."

Incomplete and misleading. Risk exists everywhere. The real danger is not understanding what risk you are taking.

"You need to be aggressive early."

In rowing, sprinting early without rhythm costs you later. Financially, chasing aggressive moves without a base creates drag that compounds.

These myths persist because they sound simple. Rowers know simple explanations often hide complex mechanics.

Saving vs Investing vs Gambling

One of the biggest sources of confusion is not knowing the difference between saving, investing, and gambling.

They are not interchangeable.

Saving is protection.

Saving is about stability, liquidity, and safety. Emergency funds. Short-term needs. Buffer against mistakes. In rowing terms, saving is staying upright. It keeps the race from ending early.

Investing is growth.

Investing is about long-term progress. Accepting volatility in exchange for compounding. Trusting time. In rowing terms, investing is settling into a sustainable race pace. You are not sprinting. You are covering distance efficiently.

Gambling is guessing.

Gambling relies on prediction, luck, and timing. It feels exciting. It feels active. Over time, it destroys rhythm. In rowing terms, gambling is randomly changing rate every 20 strokes hoping something clicks.

Many athletes are never taught these distinctions. They save too little, gamble too much, and call it investing.

That confusion creates anxiety and inconsistent behavior.

Why Athletes Pull Harder Instead of Rowing Better With Money

Athletes are conditioned to respond to struggle by increasing effort.

If the boat feels slow, pull harder.

If results lag, train more.

If pressure rises, push.

That instinct is powerful in sport.

It is dangerous with money.

When finances feel uncomfortable, people try to fix it by:

- Earning more without controlling spending

- Chasing higher returns instead of improving behavior
- Making big moves instead of fixing fundamentals

In rowing, you know what happens when someone pulls harder without staying in sync. The boat checks. Timing breaks. Efficiency drops.

Financially, the same thing happens. Pulling harder without rhythm increases stress and mistakes.

The answer is rarely more force.

It is better technique.

Why Consistency Beats Pulling Harder

Rowing rewards repeatable effort.

One great stroke does nothing.

One brutal workout does not win races.

What matters is thousands of good strokes done consistently.

Money works the same way.

Saving a little every month beats saving a lot occasionally.

Investing consistently beats timing the market.

Managing expenses quietly beats dramatic cuts followed by relapse.

Consistency creates momentum.

Momentum reduces decision fatigue.

Reduced fatigue leads to better choices.

This is where athletes actually have an advantage. You already understand this concept physically. The challenge is applying it financially without a coach enforcing it.

The Missing Coach After Competition

After rowing ends, no one is watching.

No one checks your bank balance.

No one tracks your spending.

No one corrects mistakes in real time.

Money gives delayed feedback. You can make poor decisions for years before consequences show up. That delay is why confusion persists.

Rowers are used to immediate feedback. Boat speed. Splits. Seat races. Money does not give that clarity.

This book exists to replace that missing coaching.

Coach's Perspective

A coach would not overcomplicate this.

Get the basics right.

Stop chasing quick fixes.

Row with rhythm.

Do not panic when conditions change.

Trust the process.

Effort is expected.

Discipline is required.

Consistency wins.

Game Situations and Decision Points

You start earning money after rowing.

Do you build savings first, or jump straight into investing because someone told you it was smarter?

You feel behind financially.

Do you pull harder by taking risks, or slow down and fix fundamentals?

You hear about a "can't miss" opportunity.

Do you evaluate whether it fits your long-term race plan, or chase speed?

Each decision mirrors a moment in the boat. Force or rhythm. Panic or patience.

Common Athlete Mistakes and Financial Parallels

Athletes rely on effort alone.

Financially, that leads to earning more without improving structure.

Athletes chase speed.

Financially, that leads to gambling disguised as investing.

Athletes skip fundamentals.

Financially, that creates drag that compounds quietly.

Winning the Long Race

Money feels confusing because it was never coached the way sport was.

That does not mean you missed your chance.

It means you are early in a new race.

Rowers win by respecting fundamentals, holding rhythm, and trusting the long pull. Financial success follows the same pattern. Not dramatic. Not loud. Just steady and controlled.

You do not need to pull harder.

You need to row cleaner.

Athlete Takeaways

- Money feels confusing because the structure disappeared, not because you lack discipline
- Saving, investing, and gambling are different strokes with different purposes
- Pulling harder financially often breaks rhythm instead of creating speed
- Consistency over time beats intensity every time
- Get the catch right before you worry about speed

Chapter 2: Check the Boat Set: Your Financial Snapshot

Every rower knows the feeling.

You push off the dock, take a few strokes, and something feels off. The boat is sluggish. Balance is shaky. You are working harder than you should be, but speed is not there. Before anyone talks about power or rate, the coach stops the boat.

"Check the set."

That moment is not about blame.

It is about awareness.

Until the boat is set, nothing else matters.

Your financial life works the same way.

Before investing, before big goals, before long-term strategy, you have to check the set. You need a clear snapshot of where you are right now. Not where you hope you are. Not where you think you should be. Where you actually are.

This chapter is about creating that snapshot.

Why Athletes Avoid Checking the Set Financially

Athletes are conditioned to focus forward.

Next practice.

Next race.

Next season.

Looking backward can feel uncomfortable, especially when numbers do not match expectations. Many people avoid reviewing their finances for the same reason they avoid film after a bad race. It forces honesty.

But rowing teaches this lesson early. You do not fix balance by guessing. You fix it by looking at the boat, the rigging, and the crew.

Financial clarity works the same way.

Avoidance does not protect you.

It creates drag.

Income, Expenses, and Cash Flow: The Stroke Rhythm

Cash flow is the rhythm of your financial stroke.

Income is what comes in.

Expenses are what goes out.

Cash flow is what remains.

If that rhythm is off, everything downstream struggles.

In rowing terms, income is your drive. Expenses are resistance. Cash flow is whether the boat actually moves. You can pull hard, but if resistance is high, progress is limited.

Many athletes assume income is the problem. Earn more and everything improves. Sometimes that is true. Often it is not.

Two people can earn the same amount and experience completely different outcomes based on cash flow. One feels steady. The other feels constantly behind. The difference is rhythm, not power.

Checking cash flow means answering one simple question.

At the end of the month, where does the money go?

Not in theory.

Not in intention.

In reality.

Fixed vs Variable Expenses: What Is Locked In and What Is Adjustable

Rowers understand rigging.

Some things are fixed.

Some things are adjustable.

You cannot change the length of the shell mid-practice, but you can adjust foot stretchers, oarlocks, and rate. Knowing what you can and cannot change matters.

Financially, expenses fall into two categories.

Fixed expenses are locked in.

Rent or mortgage.

Insurance.

Loan payments.

Subscriptions that never get reviewed.

Variable expenses are adjustable.

Food.

Entertainment.

Travel.

Spending habits tied to convenience or comfort.

Problems arise when everything feels fixed.

Athletes often assume their lifestyle is non-negotiable. But many "fixed" expenses were once choices that never got revisited. Over time, they harden into assumptions.

Checking the set means identifying what is truly fixed and what is simply unexamined.

You cannot adjust what you do not see.

Assets, Liabilities, and Net Worth: The Boat and the Weight in It

Assets are what help you move forward.

Liabilities are what create drag.

Net worth is the difference between the two.

This concept intimidates people because it feels like judgment. It is not. It is a measurement, nothing more.

In rowing terms, assets are clean rigging, good blades, and strong technique. Liabilities are excess weight, poor balance, and unnecessary resistance.

Net worth is not a scorecard.

It is a diagnostic tool.

Early in your career, net worth may be low or even negative. That does not mean you are failing. It means you are early in the race. What matters is trajectory, not position at one moment.

Rowers do not panic because the boat feels heavy at the start of practice. They assess and adjust.

Money deserves the same patience.

Why Net Worth Matters Even If You Feel Far From "Wealthy"

Many athletes avoid net worth because it feels irrelevant.

"I'm not wealthy."

"I don't have much yet."

"I'll deal with that later."

That thinking delays progress.

Net worth shows you whether your decisions are building or draining momentum. It reveals patterns that income alone hides. Someone earning a lot but accumulating debt is rowing hard with poor set. Someone earning modestly but building assets is rowing efficiently.

The earlier you track net worth, the more control you gain.

This is not about comparison.

It is about awareness.

Reviewing Where Your Money Actually Goes

This is the hardest part.

Intentions do not matter here.

Only evidence does.

Most people believe they know where their money goes. Few have actually reviewed it. Athletes understand this gap. You might feel like you are rowing well until film shows missed timing or rushed recovery.

Money film is bank statements and credit card transactions.

Reviewing them is uncomfortable at first. Patterns appear. Small leaks become visible. Convenience spending shows up. So do habits that no longer serve you.

This is not about cutting everything.

It is about understanding everything.

Once you see patterns, you can decide what stays and what goes.

Without review, you guess.

With review, you coach yourself.

Why This Snapshot Comes Before Strategy

Many people want to skip this chapter.

They want investing.

They want strategy.

They want growth.

Rowers know better.

You do not change rate without checking balance.

You do not push power without connection.

You do not race without knowing the boat is set.

This snapshot is not exciting.

It is essential.

It allows every future decision to be intentional instead of reactive.

Coach's Perspective

A coach would be clear.

Check the set.

Be honest.

Do not rush ahead.

Fix what you can control.

The boat tells the truth.

Numbers are not opinions.

They are feedback.

Game Situations and Decision Points

You realize your cash flow is tight.

Do you assume income is the problem, or do you review expenses first?

You see debt growing.

Do you ignore it and hope income fixes it, or do you adjust habits now?

You feel anxious about money.

Do you avoid looking, or do you gather information and regain control?

Every choice mirrors a moment in the boat. Guessing or adjusting.

Common Athlete Mistakes and Financial Parallels

Athletes avoid film after bad practices.

Financially, that means avoiding account reviews.

Athletes pull harder when the boat is off.

Financially, that means earning more without fixing cash flow.

Athletes blame conditions instead of mechanics.

Financially, that means blaming income instead of habits.

Winning the Long Race

Checking the boat set does not slow you down.

It prepares you to move efficiently.

Financial clarity removes anxiety because uncertainty disappears. Once you know where you stand, decisions become simpler. Adjustments feel manageable. Progress becomes visible.

You cannot row well in a boat you do not understand.

This chapter gives you that understanding.

Athlete Takeaways

- Cash flow is the rhythm that determines whether effort turns into progress
- Fixed and variable expenses must be identified before adjustments can happen
- Net worth is a diagnostic tool, not a judgment
- Reviewing real spending is uncomfortable but powerful
- You cannot build speed until the boat is set

Chapter 3: Establishing Rhythm: Budgeting and Saving

Every rower knows when the boat finds rhythm.

The shell feels lighter. The strokes connect. Breathing settles. You are not forcing speed, but speed shows up anyway. When rhythm is there, you can hold it for miles. When it is not, even short pieces feel exhausting.

Money works the same way.

Most people struggle financially not because they lack effort, but because they lack rhythm. Income comes in irregularly. Spending spikes emotionally. Saving happens only when it feels convenient. The result is constant correction, stress, and fatigue.

This chapter is about establishing financial rhythm. Not intensity. Not restriction. Rhythm.

Why Budgeting Feels So Unnatural to Athletes

Athletes often hate the word "budget."

It sounds restrictive.

It sounds small.

It sounds like someone telling you what you cannot do.

That reaction makes sense.

In rowing, you are not told to row less. You are taught to row better. Budgeting works the same way. A good budget is not about limiting your life. It is about directing energy efficiently so you can sustain effort over the long race.

Most budgets fail because they are built like sprints.

Too aggressive.

Too rigid.

Too disconnected from real life.

Rowers know better. You cannot sprint an entire season. You need a pace you can hold.

Budgeting Systems That Actually Work

A working budget does three things well.

It is simple.

It is repeatable.

It reflects reality, not fantasy.

In rowing terms, budgeting is your stroke rate. It sets cadence. It does not dictate power, but it controls sustainability.

There are many ways to budget. The best one is the one you will actually use.

Some people use percentage-based systems.

Some track fixed expenses and let the rest flow.

Some use envelopes or buckets.

Some use simple automation and ignore the rest.

What matters is not the system.

What matters is consistency.

A good budget answers a few core questions:

- What must be paid every month?
- What is flexible?
- What is intentionally saved?
- What is left for living?

If your budget requires daily monitoring, it will fail.

If it requires perfection, it will fail.

If it does not match your real behavior, it will fail.

Rowers adjust rate to conditions. Budgets must do the same.

Why Rhythm Beats Restriction

Many athletes approach budgeting like punishment.

Cut everything.

Restrict enjoyment.

White-knuckle discipline.

That works briefly. Then it collapses.

In rowing, restriction kills rhythm. Tight shoulders. Forced slides. Rushed recoveries. You might look disciplined, but you are wasting energy.

Financial rhythm comes from repeatable habits, not self-denial.

Saving a little every month beats saving a lot occasionally.

Spending intentionally beats cutting randomly.

Planning beats reacting.

The goal is to build a rhythm you can hold when life gets busy, stressful, or boring. Because that is most of life.

Automating Savings Like Steady Strokes

Rowers do not think about every stroke individually.

They settle into rhythm.

They trust repetition.

They let consistency do the work.

Saving should work the same way.

Automation removes decision-making. Money moves before you have time to debate it. That protects you from mood, fatigue, and impulse.

Automatic savings are like steady strokes.

They are not dramatic.

They are effective.

This includes:

- Emergency savings
- Retirement contributions
- Long-term investing
- Short-term sinking funds

When saving is automatic, progress happens quietly. You do not need motivation. You do not need discipline every day. The system carries you.

Athletes understand this principle physically.

Financially, it is the same.

Emergency Funds as Injury Protection

Every rower trains knowing injury is possible.

Not expected.

But possible.

That is why warm-ups matter.

Recovery matters.

Depth matters.

Emergency funds serve the same purpose financially.

They are not pessimism.

They are protection.

An emergency fund exists so one unexpected event does not flip the boat. Job loss. Medical issue. Car repair. Family emergency. Without reserves, people are forced into bad decisions at the worst possible time.

In rowing terms, an emergency fund keeps you upright when the water turns rough.

How much is enough depends on your situation. Income stability. Responsibilities. Risk tolerance. There is no perfect number. There is only preparedness versus exposure.

Skipping an emergency fund is like racing without knowing how to recover from a crab. You might be fine. Until you are not.

Why Athletes Resist Holding Cash

Athletes like progress.

They like movement.

They like action.

Cash feels idle.

But rowers know that recovery is not wasted time. It sets up the next stroke. Financially, cash provides flexibility. It gives you options. It allows patience instead of panic.

Emergency savings are not about returns.

They are about control.

Control keeps you in the race.

Balancing Lifestyle With Long-Term Endurance

One of the hardest financial skills is balance.

Spend too freely and you burn out later.

Restrict too much and you quit early.

Rowers understand pacing. You do not race the first 500 meters the same way you finish. You adjust effort so you can hold form across the entire course.

Financial endurance works the same way.

You should enjoy your life now.

You should also protect your future.

That balance looks different for everyone. What matters is intention. Spending should reflect values, not pressure or comparison. Saving should support future options, not create misery.

A sustainable lifestyle is one you do not resent.

Why Lifestyle Inflation Breaks Rhythm

As income increases, spending often follows.

Bigger apartment.

Better car.

More convenience.

None of these are wrong. They become problems when they happen automatically instead of intentionally.

In rowing, adding power without balance creates instability. Financially, increasing spending without adjusting savings breaks rhythm.

The goal is not to freeze lifestyle.

It is to scale intentionally.

Every increase should ask one question.

Does this improve endurance or just add drag?

Coach's Perspective

A coach would keep it simple.

Find your rhythm.

Do not rush.

Be consistent.

Protect yourself.

Hold form when it gets uncomfortable.

Nobody sprints a season.

Nobody wings a budget and wins long-term.

Game Situations and Decision Points

You get a raise.

Do you increase spending immediately, or adjust savings first?

You feel stressed about money.

Do you cut everything suddenly, or build a system you can maintain?

An unexpected expense hits.

Do you panic and borrow, or lean on your emergency fund?

Each decision mirrors a moment in the boat. Force or rhythm.

Common Athlete Mistakes and Financial Parallels

Athletes train too hard without recovery.

Financially, that means overspending without saving.

Athletes ignore pacing.

Financially, that means lifestyle inflation without endurance.

Athletes rely on motivation.

Financially, that means inconsistent saving.

Winning the Long Race

Rhythm is what carries you when effort fades.

Budgeting and saving are not about control. They are about freedom. When rhythm exists, money becomes predictable instead of stressful. Decisions become easier. Progress becomes visible.

You do not need to pull harder.

You need to hold rate.

Establish rhythm early, and the rest of the race becomes manageable.

Athlete Takeaways

- Budgeting sets financial rhythm, not restriction
- Systems that work are simple, repeatable, and realistic
- Automating savings builds progress without daily effort
- Emergency funds keep you upright in rough water
- Sustainable pacing beats short-term intensity every time

Chapter 4: Drag Factor Decisions: Credit and Debt

Every rower understands drag.

You feel it immediately. The shell does not accelerate the way it should. The boat feels heavy. You can increase power, but the speed does not respond. Something is slowing you down, even if you cannot see it clearly from your seat.

Before changing rate or pulling harder, a good coach checks drag factors. Rigging. Set. Resistance. Anything that quietly steals efficiency.

Credit and debt work the same way in your financial life.

They are not inherently bad. Used correctly, they can help the boat move. Used poorly, they create drag that compounds quietly over time. This chapter is about learning how credit works, how debt affects speed, and how to make decisions that reduce resistance instead of adding it.

Why Credit Feels Confusing to Athletes

Athletes are taught to train, not to borrow.

Credit is rarely explained clearly. Most people learn about it through trial and error. A card arrives in the mail. A loan is approved. Payments are set. The system works, but the mechanics stay hidden.

Rowers would never accept that approach in the boat.

You would not row without understanding rigging. You would not race without knowing the course. Credit deserves the same respect. When you understand how it works, you can use it intentionally. When you do not, it controls pace without your permission.

How Credit Scores and Reports Actually Work

A credit score is a summary, not a judgment.

It is a numerical snapshot that lenders use to estimate risk. It does not measure intelligence or worth. It measures behavior over time.

In rowing terms, a credit score is like split times averaged over many pieces. One bad stroke does not ruin it. Repeated mistakes do.

Your credit report is the full film.

Your credit score is the highlight number.

Several factors influence that score.

Payment history matters most.

Did you make payments on time? Late payments create drag immediately.

Utilization matters.

How much of your available credit are you using? High utilization signals strain, even if you pay on time.

Length of history matters.

Longer, stable history helps. New accounts shorten the visible track record.

New credit matters.

Frequent applications signal instability.

Mix matters.

Different types of credit show versatility, but this is a minor factor compared to consistency.

Rowers understand that rhythm over time matters more than one hard pull. Credit rewards the same behavior.

Credit Cards, Loans, and Interest: Understanding Resistance

Credit is a tool.

Interest is the cost of using it.

Credit cards are short-term tools designed for convenience. When paid in full, they can be efficient. When balances carry, interest creates heavy drag.

Loans are longer-term tools. Mortgages. Student loans. Auto loans. They spread cost over time. That can be useful or dangerous depending on structure.

Interest is resistance.

In rowing terms, interest is like rowing against current. You can still move forward, but every stroke requires more effort. The higher the interest rate, the stronger the current.

Ignoring interest is like ignoring water conditions. You might feel strong, but resistance quietly drains progress.

Why Athletes Misuse Credit Cards

Athletes are comfortable with effort.

They are less comfortable with delayed consequences.

Credit cards offer immediate convenience and delayed cost. That combination is dangerous. Small balances feel manageable. Minimum payments feel harmless. Over time, interest compounds against you.

Rowers would never accept repeated small technique errors because they know those errors show up later in the race. Credit card misuse works the same way.

Using cards without a system creates drag that builds invisibly.

Good Debt vs Bad Debt: A Useful but Incomplete Framework

People often label debt as "good" or "bad."

That language helps, but it oversimplifies.

Good debt generally supports growth or stability.

Bad debt generally supports consumption.

But context matters.

A mortgage with manageable payments can support long-term stability.

The same mortgage with stretched payments creates pressure.

Student loans that lead to increased earning power may be productive.

The same loans without a plan create long-term drag.

Credit card debt used temporarily and paid quickly may be manageable.

The same debt carried indefinitely becomes destructive.

In rowing terms, weight is not automatically bad. Where it sits, how it moves, and how it affects balance matters.

Debt is not about labels.

It is about impact.

Ask better questions.

Does this debt increase future flexibility?

Does it support income or stability?

Can it be serviced without strain?

Does it reduce options later?

If the answers trend negative, drag is building.

How Debt Slows the Shell Over Time

Debt creates three types of drag.

Cash flow drag.

Monthly payments reduce flexibility. Less room to adjust. Less margin for error.

Mental drag.

Stress, anxiety, and distraction increase when obligations pile up.

Opportunity drag.

Money tied to payments cannot be redirected to opportunities or protection.

Rowers feel this immediately. A heavy boat responds slower to changes. Financially, debt-heavy situations reduce responsiveness. Small problems become big because flexibility is gone.

This is why debt decisions deserve patience.

Common Debt Mistakes Athletes Make

Athletes often make the same mistakes with debt because they rely on familiar instincts.

Pulling harder instead of rowing cleaner.

Earning more instead of fixing spending patterns.

Focusing on monthly payments instead of total cost.

Longer loans feel easier but increase drag.

Using credit to smooth lifestyle instead of building rhythm.

Temporary relief becomes permanent resistance.

Avoiding review because it feels uncomfortable.

Ignoring drag does not remove it.

Rowers know that ignoring set never fixes balance. Money is no different.

How to Reduce Drag Without Panic

Reducing debt does not require extreme measures.

It requires clarity and order.

List balances.

List rates.

Understand minimums.

Identify highest resistance first.

This is not about shame.

It is about mechanics.

Rowers adjust technique calmly. Financial adjustments should feel the same. Gradual improvements compound.

Sometimes the best move is not aggressive payoff.

Sometimes it is restructuring.

Sometimes it is stopping new drag from being added.

The right answer depends on the full boat, not one seat.

Why Zero Debt Is Not the Only Goal

Some athletes believe the only safe position is zero debt.

That is not always realistic or optimal.

Rowers know that equipment, travel, and training cost money. The goal is not to eliminate cost. It is to ensure cost supports performance.

Financially, the goal is not debt elimination at any cost.

The goal is control.

Debt that is understood, manageable, and intentional can coexist with progress. Debt that controls decisions cannot.

Control is the real finish line.

Coach's Perspective

A coach would be blunt.

Check your drag.

Do not ignore resistance.

Fix technique before adding power.

Details matter.

You cannot outwork drag forever.

Effort without efficiency breaks crews.

Money works the same way.

Game Situations and Decision Points

You qualify for more credit.

Do you ask whether it helps the boat or adds resistance?

You feel behind financially.

Do you pull harder by borrowing, or slow down and reduce drag?

A payment feels manageable today.

Do you consider long-term impact or only short-term relief?

Every decision mirrors a stroke choice. Clean connection or wasted effort.

Common Athlete Mistakes and Financial Parallels

Athletes rely on strength to cover technique flaws.

Financially, that means earning more without fixing debt.

Athletes rush adjustments.

Financially, that means consolidating or borrowing without understanding terms.

Athletes ignore small inefficiencies.

Financially, that allows drag to compound quietly.

Winning the Long Race

Credit and debt decisions shape how the boat feels over distance.

When drag is managed, rhythm holds. Adjustments are easier. Confidence increases. When drag is ignored, every stroke costs more than it should.

You do not need to eliminate every ounce of resistance.

You need to understand it and manage it intentionally.

Rowers win long races by reducing drag before increasing power.

Money rewards the same discipline.

Athlete Takeaways

- Credit scores reflect rhythm and consistency, not worth
- Interest is resistance that compounds quietly
- Debt should support stability or growth, not strain
- Monthly payments hide long-term drag
- Reduce resistance before pulling harder

Chapter 5: The Boathouse of Money: Banking Basics

Every rowing program has a boathouse.

It is not glamorous. It does not win races by itself. But without it, nothing works. Boats are stored there. Oars are rigged there. Repairs happen there. Systems are checked there. The boathouse is where order lives so performance can happen on the water.

Banking plays the same role in your financial life.

It is the infrastructure that supports everything else. Income flows through it. Bills get paid there. Savings are held there. Transfers happen there. When banking is set up poorly, everything feels harder than it should. When it is set up well, money moves smoothly and quietly in the background.

This chapter is about understanding the boathouse of your money and making sure it is built for function, not frustration.

Why Athletes Overlook Banking

Athletes are trained to focus on performance, not infrastructure.

You show up to practice and the boat is ready. Oars are set. Launches are fueled. You rarely think about what makes that possible. Banking often gets treated the same way. Something necessary, but not worth attention unless something goes wrong.

That is a mistake.

Rowers know that small boathouse problems create big on-water issues. A damaged oarlock. Poorly maintained rigging. Missing equipment. Banking works the same way. Minor inefficiencies quietly add stress, fees, and mistakes.

Understanding banking basics gives you control before problems appear.

Checking vs Savings Accounts: Different Bays, Different Purposes

In a boathouse, not everything is stored in the same place.

Boats go in racks.

Oars go in slings.

Tools go in lockers.

Each space has a purpose. Mixing them creates chaos.

Checking and savings accounts serve different roles.

A checking account is for movement.

This is where income lands. Bills get paid. Transfers happen. It is designed for frequent use.

A savings account is for holding.

This is where money waits. Emergency funds. Short-term goals. Buffers. It is not designed for daily activity.

Problems arise when these roles blur.

Using checking for everything leads to spending money that should be protected.

Using savings like checking defeats its purpose and creates temptation.

Rowers understand this intuitively. You do not store race shells where they can get damaged by daily traffic. Financially, savings deserves the same separation.

Why Separation Matters for Discipline

Athletes rely on structure.

In rowing, structure reduces decision-making. You know where to be. What to use. How to prepare. Banking structure does the same thing.

When savings is separate:

- Spending decisions become clearer
- Emergency money feels less accessible
- Discipline becomes easier without extra effort

This is not about restriction.

It is about clarity.

Clear systems reduce mistakes when attention is elsewhere.

Online Banks vs Traditional Banks: Choosing the Right Facility

Not all boathouses are the same.

Some are old, solid, and familiar.

Some are newer, streamlined, and efficient.

Both can work. The choice depends on needs.

Traditional banks offer physical locations.

You can walk in. Talk to someone. Handle cash easily. For some people, that familiarity matters.

Online banks offer efficiency.

Higher interest rates on savings. Fewer fees. Cleaner digital tools. Faster transfers.

Many athletes benefit from using both.

Traditional banks for:

- Cash deposits
- In-person needs
- Legacy accounts

Online banks for:

- Emergency savings
- High-yield savings
- Automated systems

In rowing terms, this is using different facilities for different purposes. You do not rig boats in the launch ramp. You use the right space for the right job.

Fees: The Quiet Leak in the Boathouse

Rowers hate leaks.

A slow leak ruins sessions. Water builds quietly. Performance suffers before anyone notices.

Bank fees work the same way.

Monthly maintenance fees.

Overdraft fees.

ATM fees.

Transfer fees.

Individually, they feel small. Over time, they add drag and frustration. Many people pay these fees simply because they never reviewed their setup.

Athletes would never accept leaking shells without fixing them. Financially, the same discipline applies.

If a bank charges you for basic access to your own money, that deserves scrutiny.

How Money Moves Electronically: Understanding the Current

Modern money rarely moves physically.

Direct deposit.

Automatic payments.

Transfers.

Apps.

Peer-to-peer services.

Money moves electronically like current moves under the shell. You may not see it, but it affects everything.

Understanding how money moves protects you from mistakes.

Direct deposit ensures income arrives automatically.

Automatic bill pay reduces missed payments.

Transfers allow money to flow between systems.

Apps increase convenience but also risk.

Rowers respect current because ignoring it leads to steering errors. Financially, ignoring how money moves creates confusion and overdrafts.

Know:

- When deposits hit
- When bills clear
- How long transfers take
- What happens if timing is off

Timing matters more than people realize.

Overdrafts: The Financial Crab

Every rower knows the feeling of catching a crab.

Sudden.

Embarrassing.

Costly.

Overdrafts are financial crabs.

You spend money you thought was there.

A charge hits earlier than expected.

A transfer arrives late.

Fees stack quickly.

Overdrafts are rarely about irresponsibility. They are about poor timing and unclear systems.

Protection matters.

You can:

- Keep buffers in checking
- Link savings for overdraft protection
- Set alerts for low balances

- Space bill due dates

In rowing terms, this is learning how to recover quickly instead of panicking. Preparation prevents capsizing.

Fraud and Financial Safety: Protecting the Boathouse

Boathouses are secured for a reason.

Locks.

Cameras.

Access control.

Money needs protection too.

Fraud is real.

Identity theft happens.

Scams target convenience and urgency.

Protecting yourself does not require paranoia.

It requires awareness.

Basic protections include:

- Strong, unique passwords
- Two-factor authentication
- Monitoring accounts regularly
- Avoiding unknown links and urgent requests
- Keeping personal information limited

Athletes understand protecting equipment. Money deserves the same respect.

If something feels rushed or secretive, step back. Legitimate systems do not require panic.

Why Banking Problems Create Emotional Stress

Banking issues feel personal.

Missed payments.

Fees.

Fraud alerts.

Account freezes.

They trigger frustration and anxiety because money is tied to safety. When banking is chaotic, everything else feels unstable.

Rowers know that instability affects performance. When the shell feels off, confidence drops. Financial stability begins in the boathouse, not in the race.

Clean systems create calm.

Setting Up a Functional Financial Boathouse

A good banking setup does not need to be complex.

It needs to be intentional.

At minimum:

- One checking account for income and bills
- One savings account for emergencies
- Automated deposits and payments
- Alerts for balances and activity
- Minimal fees

This setup supports rhythm without constant attention.

Once systems are in place, you can focus on bigger goals without worrying about basics falling apart.

Coach's Perspective

A coach would not debate this.

Take care of your equipment.

Fix small problems early.

Do not ignore leaks.

Protect the boathouse.

You cannot row well from a broken foundation.

Game Situations and Decision Points

You notice fees each month.

Do you ignore them or fix the setup?

You overdraft occasionally.

Do you blame timing or build buffers?

You use multiple apps.

Do you track money flow or hope it works?

Every decision affects stability.

Common Athlete Mistakes and Financial Parallels

Athletes ignore infrastructure.

Financially, that means messy banking.

Athletes assume small issues do not matter.

Financially, that allows fees and overdrafts to compound.

Athletes react late.

Financially, that increases stress.

Winning the Long Race

Banking does not create wealth.

It supports everything that does.

When the boathouse is organized, rowing improves. When banking is set up correctly, financial decisions feel lighter and more controlled.

You do not need a perfect system.

You need a functional one.

Set the foundation.

Protect the infrastructure.

Let money move smoothly in the background.

Athlete Takeaways

- Checking and savings accounts serve different roles and should stay separate
- Banking systems should reduce effort, not require constant attention
- Fees and overdrafts are leaks that slow progress
- Understanding how money moves prevents mistakes
- A clean financial boathouse creates calm and control

Part II: Balance, Protection, and Staying Upright

One mistake can flip the boat.

Every rower has felt it.

The boat is moving well. Rhythm is solid. Then one rushed stroke, one moment of lost balance, and suddenly everything is unstable. Oars clash. The shell rocks. Sometimes you recover. Sometimes you swim.

Rowing does not forgive carelessness.

Financially, the same principle applies. You can do many things right and still get knocked off course by one unprotected risk. An injury. An accident. A lawsuit. A health issue. A major loss without a buffer. Progress disappears quickly when protection is missing.

This section of the book is about staying upright.

Why Balance Matters More Than Speed

Rowers understand balance before power.

A balanced boat transfers effort efficiently. An unbalanced boat wastes energy and magnifies mistakes. Protection in rowing is not passive. It is awareness. Proper set. Clean recovery. Respect for conditions.

Financial balance works the same way.

You can have strong income.

You can be saving consistently.

You can be investing intelligently.

Without protection, one unexpected event can undo years of work. Balance is what allows progress to continue after mistakes or surprises.

This section teaches you how to protect momentum.

Risk Is Part of the Race

Rowers accept risk.

Weather changes.

Equipment fails.

Bodies break down.

The goal is not to eliminate risk. It is to understand it and prepare for it. Ignoring risk does not make it disappear. It makes consequences worse.

Financial risk works the same way.

Health risks.

Income risks.

Legal risks.

Property risks.

You cannot control every variable, but you can prepare for many of them. Protection is not pessimism. It is professionalism.

Staying Upright Requires Awareness

In rowing, staying upright requires constant micro-adjustments.

Pressure changes.

Balance shifts.

Conditions vary.

You do not panic.

You adapt.

Financial protection requires the same mindset. Insurance. Emergency funds. Liability coverage. These tools exist so small mistakes do not end the race.

Athletes often underestimate risk because they are healthy, capable, and resilient. That mindset works in training. It fails financially when randomness shows up.

Balance protects progress.

Protection Is Not Fear-Based

Many people avoid insurance and protection because it feels negative.

They think preparing for bad outcomes invites them.

Rowers know better.

You do not practice recovery drills because you expect to flip. You practice them so flipping does not end the session. Financial protection serves the same purpose.

It keeps you rowing when things go wrong.

How This Section Fits Into the Bigger Plan

Part I built your foundation.

Cash flow.

Saving rhythm.

Basic systems.

Part II protects that foundation.

You will learn how to:

- Think clearly about risk
- Protect income and assets
- Avoid common insurance mistakes
- Stay balanced when life changes

This section is not about optimization.

It is about survival.

Survival creates confidence.

Confidence allows progress.

A Coach's Perspective

A coach would not sugarcoat this.

Respect the water.

Stay balanced.

Protect yourself.

One bad stroke can flip the boat.

Preparation keeps you in the race.

You do not win by ignoring risk.

You win by managing it.

Why Athletes Often Skip Protection

Athletes are used to pushing through pain.

They assume resilience solves problems. Financially, resilience without protection leads to exposure. You can grind through a workout. You cannot grind through a lawsuit or medical bill without preparation.

Skipping protection is like racing without knowing how to recover from a crab. It works until it does not.

What Staying Upright Allows

When protection is in place:

- You take smarter risks
- You stay calm during chaos
- You avoid forced decisions
- You protect long-term goals

Rowers know that confidence comes from preparation, not denial. Financial confidence works the same way.

Winning the Long Race

Balance keeps you in the boat.

Protection keeps you moving forward even when mistakes happen. You do not need perfect conditions. You need the ability to recover.

Part II is about giving you that ability.

Set the boat.

Respect the water.

Stay upright.

The race is long.

Preparation makes it survivable.

Chapter 6: Risk Awareness and Staying in Sync

Every rower learns this early.

You can have strong athletes, perfect conditioning, and a fast shell, but if the crew is not in sync, speed disappears. Worse, instability creeps in. The boat feels heavy. Timing breaks down. Small mistakes become big ones.

Risk works the same way.

It is not just about strength or effort. It is about awareness, timing, and knowing when to apply pressure and when to steady the boat. Most financial mistakes happen not because people take risk, but because they misunderstand it.

This chapter is about learning to stay in sync with risk instead of fighting it.

Opening Story From the Sport

Imagine a race where conditions are changing.

The water is choppy.

A headwind kicks up.

Your crew feels strong and wants to push.

One rower starts pulling harder.

Another shortens the stroke to keep balance.

A third rushes the slide to gain speed.

Individually, everyone is trying to help. Collectively, the boat slows down.

The coach does not yell for more power.

The coach yells for rhythm.

Risk awareness in money works exactly the same way.

Emotional Risk vs Financial Risk

Athletes are comfortable with physical risk.

You train through discomfort.

You race tired.

You accept pain as part of progress.

Emotional risk feels different.

Emotion shows up as fear, excitement, impatience, or overconfidence. Financial decisions are often driven by emotion, not logic. That is where athletes get tripped up.

Financial risk is the measurable part.

Volatility.

Loss potential.

Time horizon.

Probability.

Emotional risk is how you feel about those things.

In rowing terms, financial risk is water conditions. Emotional risk is how panicked you get when the boat rocks.

You cannot control the water.

You can control your response.

Many athletes confuse discomfort with danger. A wobbly boat feels scary, but it does not mean you are flipping. Markets feel the same way. Movement does not equal failure.

Time Horizon and Flexibility

Rowers think in race distance.

A 2K race is different from a long training row.

You pace differently.

You apply pressure at different moments.

Time horizon is your financial race distance.

If you need money soon, risk tolerance is lower. The boat needs to be stable. If the finish line is far away, you can afford more movement and more pressure.

Flexibility matters too.

If you have stable income, emergency reserves, and time, you can absorb volatility. If you lack flexibility, even small setbacks feel catastrophic.

In rowing terms, flexibility is water depth and room to adjust. Shallow water requires caution. Open water allows more aggression.

Risk is never isolated. It always connects to time and flexibility.

How Risk Affects Every Money Decision

Risk is not just an investing concept.

It affects:

- Spending decisions
- Career moves
- Debt choices
- Insurance coverage
- Savings strategies

Every financial decision either increases or decreases risk exposure.

Taking on debt increases risk.

Skipping emergency savings increases risk.

Relying on one income source increases risk.

Risk awareness means understanding how decisions stack.

In rowing terms, this is cumulative fatigue. One bad stroke may not matter. Repeated mistakes compound until the boat breaks down.

Athletes often focus on the big risks and ignore the small ones. Financially, small unmanaged risks are often the most dangerous.

Knowing When to Push and When to Steady

Great crews know when to apply pressure.

They push during favorable conditions.

They steady during rough water.

They never panic.

Financially, this means understanding context.

There are times to be aggressive.

There are times to protect position.

There are times to do nothing.

Pushing when conditions are wrong leads to mistakes. Steadying too long leads to stagnation.

In rowing terms, you do not sprint through rough water. You do not coast when the shell is running.

Risk awareness is situational awareness.

Common Athlete Misunderstandings About Risk

Athletes often believe:

- Harder effort fixes everything
- Confidence equals safety
- Youth eliminates consequences

These beliefs break down financially.

You cannot outwork bad timing.

Confidence does not remove downside.

Time only helps if you stay in the boat.

Risk does not care how tough you are. It only cares whether you prepared.

Coach's Perspective

What would your coach say?

Stay in sync.
Respect the conditions.
Don't rush the slide.
Control what you can control.
Don't panic.
Trust the rhythm.
Smart pressure wins races.
A coach would never tell you to row scared.
They would also never tell you to row reckless.
Discipline lives between those extremes.

Game Situations and Decision Points

Situation 1

Markets drop suddenly.
Do you pull harder out of fear, or steady the boat and trust the race plan?
Financially, reacting emotionally often locks in mistakes.

Situation 2

Your income increases.
Do you take on more obligations immediately, or increase flexibility first?
Financially, growth without stability increases risk.

Situation 3

A new opportunity appears.
Do you evaluate timing and impact, or jump because it feels exciting?
Financially, excitement without context leads to imbalance.
Each decision either improves sync or disrupts it.

Common Athlete Mistakes and Financial Parallels

Athletes rush the stroke.

Financially, that shows up as chasing returns.

Athletes ignore conditions.

Financially, that shows up as poor timing.

Athletes rely on toughness alone.

Financially, that shows up as underestimating risk.

Athletes row out of sync.

Financially, that shows up as misaligned decisions.

Winning the Long Race

Risk is not the enemy.

Unmanaged risk is.

The goal is not to eliminate movement. It is to stay upright while moving forward. Athletes who understand risk develop patience, discipline, and confidence that transfers beyond sport.

You do not win by avoiding rough water.

You win by staying composed through it.

Risk awareness keeps the boat moving when others flip.

Athlete Takeaways

- Risk is about timing and awareness, not fear
- Emotional reactions disrupt rhythm faster than bad conditions
- Time horizon and flexibility determine how much pressure you can apply
- Smart crews know when to push and when to steady
- Staying in sync matters more than pulling harder

Chapter 7: Insurance Fundamentals Every Rower Needs

Every rower knows this truth, even if it is rarely said out loud.

You can train perfectly.

You can race smart.

You can execute your plan.

And still, things happen.

An oar catches a crab.

A teammate gets hurt.

Weather shifts unexpectedly.

Equipment fails.

Insurance exists for the same reason safety launches exist. You hope you never need them, but the day you do, everything depends on having them in place.

This chapter is not about fear.

It is about protection.

It is about staying upright when conditions change.

Opening Story From the Sport

Picture a long training row.

Conditions are calm.

The crew feels smooth.

Everything is clicking.

Then someone catches a bad crab.

The boat lurches.

Momentum stops.

One mistake threatens the entire shell.

Now imagine there is no launch nearby.

No backup plan.

No way to respond.

That is what life looks like without insurance.

Insurance does not make you faster.

It keeps one moment from ending the race.

What Insurance Really Is

Athletes often misunderstand insurance.

They see it as wasted money.

Something you pay for but hope never to use.

A cost without upside.

In reality, insurance is risk transfer.

You are paying to shift the financial impact of rare but severe events away from yourself. You are not buying a return. You are buying stability.

In rowing terms, insurance is boat rigging and safety checks. It does not win races. It prevents disasters.

Ignoring insurance is not confidence.

It is exposure.

Health Insurance Basics

Health insurance is foundational.

Injuries and illness are not hypothetical. They are part of life. Without coverage, medical costs can derail everything you are building.

Health insurance typically includes:

- Monthly premiums

- Deductibles
- Copays or coinsurance
- Out-of-pocket maximums

In rowing terms, this is your medical staff and recovery plan.

Premiums are the cost of having access.

Deductibles are how much you absorb before help kicks in.

Out-of-pocket maximums are the limit to how bad it can get.

Young athletes often assume they do not need strong coverage because they feel healthy. That logic fails the first time something unexpected happens.

Health insurance protects your ability to keep rowing, not just your health.

Auto and Renters Insurance

Auto insurance is mandatory for a reason.

Cars move fast.

Mistakes happen.

Damage extends beyond your vehicle.

Auto insurance covers:

- Liability to others
- Damage to your vehicle
- Medical costs related to accidents

In rowing terms, this is collision avoidance and shared water responsibility. You are not just protecting yourself. You are protecting everyone around you.

Renters insurance is one of the most overlooked protections.

It covers:

- Personal property
- Liability
- Temporary housing after a loss

Many athletes skip renters insurance because they underestimate what they own. Equipment, electronics, clothing, and personal items add up quickly.

Renters insurance is cheap.

Replacing everything is not.

Homeowners Insurance

Homeownership changes the equation.

You are no longer just protecting belongings.

You are protecting a structure.

Land.

Liability tied to the property.

Homeowners insurance typically covers:

- The home itself
- Personal property
- Liability
- Additional living expenses if the home is unlivable

In rowing terms, this is protecting the boathouse, not just the shell.

Homeownership comes with responsibility. Insurance is not optional protection. It is required discipline.

Underinsuring a home to save money is like rowing with damaged riggers. It works until it doesn't.

Deductibles, Premiums, and Coverage Limits

This is where many athletes get confused.

Premiums are what you pay regularly.

Deductibles are what you pay when something happens.

Coverage limits are the maximum protection.

Lower premiums usually mean higher deductibles.

Higher coverage limits usually mean higher premiums.

There is no perfect setup.

In rowing terms, this is choosing between lighter equipment and durability. Lighter setups move faster but tolerate less error. Heavier setups are more forgiving.

The right balance depends on:

- Cash reserves
- Income stability
- Risk tolerance
- Stage of life

The mistake is choosing the cheapest option without understanding exposure.

Cheap coverage that fails under pressure is not protection.

Why Athletes Often Get This Wrong

Athletes are conditioned to accept risk.

You train through pain.

You play through discomfort.

You trust your body.

That mindset does not translate well to insurance.

Insurance is not about toughness.

It is about math.

One accident can undo years of discipline if protection is missing or insufficient.

In rowing terms, grit does not fix a flipped shell.

Coach's Perspective

What would your coach say?

Handle your business.

Protect the boat.

We don't take unnecessary risks.
Prepare for what you can't control.
Stay upright.
A coach would never skip safety checks to save time.
They would never race without a launch nearby.
Insurance is part of preparation, not pessimism.

Game Situations and Decision Points

Situation 1

You are young and healthy.

Do you skip health insurance or choose a plan that protects against worst-case scenarios?

Financially, youth reduces probability, not impact.

Situation 2

You rent and own little furniture.

Do you skip renters insurance or protect against total loss?

Financially, replacement costs show up fast.

Situation 3

You buy a home.

Do you underinsure to save money or protect the full value?

Financially, partial coverage creates full stress.

Each choice either limits damage or amplifies it.

Common Athlete Mistakes and Financial Parallels

Athletes underestimate injury risk.

Financially, that means inadequate health coverage.

Athletes ignore off-field preparation.

Financially, that means missing renters or liability coverage.

Athletes chase efficiency over safety.

Financially, that means choosing the cheapest policy blindly.

Athletes assume nothing will happen.

Financially, that assumption is expensive.

Winning the Long Race

Insurance does not make progress.

It preserves it.

It allows you to train, work, and build without one event wiping out years of effort. Athletes who respect protection stay in the race longer.

You do not win by tempting disaster.

You win by staying upright through uncertainty.

Athlete Takeaways

- Insurance is risk transfer, not wasted money
- Health insurance protects your ability to keep rowing
- Auto and renters insurance prevent one mistake from becoming a setback
- Homeowners insurance protects long-term stability
- Smart coverage keeps the shell upright when conditions change

Chapter 8: Life, Disability, and Liability Protection

Every experienced rower knows the difference between speed and survivability.

You can have a fast shell.

You can have strong athletes.

You can even have perfect technique.

But without depth, backup plans, and protection, one problem can end the race.

Life, disability, and liability insurance are not exciting topics. They do not feel urgent when things are going well. That is exactly why they matter. They are not about racing today. They are about making sure one unexpected moment does not erase years of work.

Rowers understand this intuitively. You do not row a long race assuming nothing will go wrong. You plan for fatigue, weather changes, equipment issues, and human error.

This chapter is about building that same mindset into your financial life.

Opening Story From the Sport

Think about a long regatta day.

Multiple races.

Changing conditions.

Bodies wearing down.

The crews that survive the day are not just the fastest. They are the ones with depth. Athletes who can step in. Equipment that can be swapped. Coaches who plan beyond the first race.

The crews that assume everything will go perfectly rarely finish strong.

Life insurance, disability insurance, and liability coverage are financial depth. They do not help when everything goes right. They save you when something goes wrong.

What These Coverages Actually Protect

Most athletes misunderstand these protections because they focus on the wrong thing.

They think life insurance is about death.

They think disability insurance is about catastrophic injury.

They think liability insurance is about unlikely lawsuits.

In reality, all three protect continuity.

They protect people who depend on you.

They protect income that supports your life.

They protect assets you are building.

In rowing terms, they protect the race plan from one unexpected disruption.

Term vs Permanent Life Insurance

Life insurance exists to protect others from financial harm if you are not there.

If no one depends on your income, life insurance may not be a priority yet.

If someone would struggle financially without you, life insurance matters.

That is the purpose. Nothing more.

Term Life Insurance

Term life insurance covers you for a specific period of time.

Common terms are 10, 20, or 30 years.

It is:

- Simple
- Affordable
- Designed for income replacement

Term insurance is often the right starting point for athletes and young professionals. It covers the years when financial responsibility is highest.

In rowing terms, term insurance is your race-day lineup. It is built for the conditions you know are coming.

Permanent Life Insurance

Permanent life insurance lasts your entire life and includes additional features such as cash value.

It is:

- More complex
- More expensive
- Highly dependent on proper design

Permanent insurance can make sense in specific situations. Estate planning. Long-term dependents. Advanced tax planning. It is not automatically better.

In rowing terms, permanent insurance is specialized equipment. It has a role, but only when the fundamentals are already strong.

Installing complexity before basics are established slows the shell.

Disability Insurance and Income Protection

This is the most overlooked protection for athletes.

Your income funds everything.

Housing.

Food.

Savings.

Insurance itself.

Disability insurance protects your ability to earn if injury or illness prevents you from working.

Most people are far more likely to experience a period of disability than premature death. Yet many skip this coverage entirely.

In rowing terms, this is protecting the engine.

You can replace equipment.

You can adjust lineups.

You cannot replace your earning ability easily.

Disability insurance replaces a portion of income, not all of it. The goal is stability, not luxury. It keeps the race from ending when you cannot pull.

Athletes often assume toughness will carry them through anything. That mindset works on the water. It fails financially.

You cannot grind through a medical condition that prevents you from working.

Umbrella Liability Coverage

Liability risk grows quietly.

As income increases.

As assets accumulate.

As responsibilities expand.

Umbrella insurance provides additional liability protection on top of auto and homeowners insurance.

It covers situations where basic policies are not enough.

Lawsuits do not require wrongdoing.

They require accusations.

They require opportunity.

They require assets.

In rowing terms, umbrella coverage is the safety launch that stays back but moves fast when something breaks down.

You hope you never need it.

When you do, nothing else replaces it.

Umbrella coverage is usually inexpensive relative to the protection it provides. That alone should tell you something.

How These Protections Work Together

Life insurance protects people.

Disability insurance protects income.

Liability insurance protects assets.

Each covers a different risk. Skipping one leaves exposure somewhere else.

In rowing terms, this is seat balance.

Strong pullers mean nothing if the shell is unstable.

Protection works as a system, not as isolated pieces.

Common Insurance Mistakes Athletes Make

Athletes tend to repeat the same mistakes because of how they are conditioned.

Mistake One: Assuming Youth Equals Safety

Feeling strong does not reduce financial impact.

It only reduces perceived urgency.

Risk does not ask permission.

Mistake Two: Insuring Stuff Instead of Income

Phones, cars, and gear get insured.
Income often does not.
That is backwards.

Mistake Three: Buying Based on Cost Alone

Cheapest coverage often fails when tested.
Low premiums hide high exposure.

Mistake Four: Overcomplicating Early

Permanent insurance before dependents.
Complex strategies before stability.
That is pulling harder instead of rowing smoother.

Mistake Five: Never Updating Coverage

Life changes.
Income changes.
Responsibilities change.
Protection must evolve.

Coach's Perspective

What would your coach say?
Protect the boat.
Protect the crew.
Do not assume conditions stay calm.
Prepare for the whole race.
Handle your business.
A coach would never send a crew out without safety protocols. Financial

protection is no different.

Game Situations and Decision Points

Situation 1

You are single and early in your career.

Do you ignore disability coverage or protect your income early?

Financially, early protection is cheaper and easier.

Situation 2

You start a family.

Do you assume nothing will happen or protect dependents intentionally?

Financially, delay increases risk.

Situation 3

Your income grows.

Do you keep minimal liability limits or adjust protection?

Financially, exposure rises quietly.

Each decision either adds stability or increases fragility.

The Long Race Reality

Rowing teaches patience.

You do not sprint the first 500 meters.

You do not ignore technique under fatigue.

You do not assume calm water stays calm.

Life and money work the same way.

Life, disability, and liability insurance do not make you rich.

They keep you from becoming fragile.

They keep the race going when conditions change.

Athlete Takeaways

- Life insurance protects people who depend on you
- Term coverage is usually the right first stroke
- Disability insurance protects the engine that drives everything
- Umbrella coverage protects assets as the race gets longer
- Smart protection keeps you rowing when others flip

Part III: Building Speed (Investing Fundamentals)

Speed comes from efficiency, not panic.

Every rower eventually reaches a point where effort alone stops working.

Early on, speed feels simple. Pull harder. Raise the rate. Push through fatigue. The boat responds for a while, then something breaks down. The shell loses run. Timing slips. Technique deteriorates. What felt powerful becomes inefficient.

The fastest crews learn a different lesson.

Speed is not about pulling harder.

It is about pulling better.

Investing works the same way.

Many people believe financial progress comes from intensity. More trades. More adjustments. More reactions to news and market moves. That activity feels productive, but over time it slows progress. Wealth is built the same way boats move fastest. Through clean execution, consistency, and efficiency.

This part of the book is about learning how to build speed without panic.

Why Panic Feels Like Action

In rowing, panic often shows up when conditions change. Rough water. A bad start. A missed call. Athletes rush the catch, shorten the stroke, and spike the rate. The boat feels frantic and slow at the same time.

Financial panic looks identical.

Checking accounts constantly.

Reacting to market drops.

Chasing what just performed well.

Abandoning plans during volatility.

All of this feels like doing something. Very little of it creates forward motion.

Markets are not impressed by urgency. They reward discipline. Investors who move fastest over time are rarely the most active. They are the most consistent.

Efficiency Beats Effort Over Long Distances

Rowers do not measure success by exhaustion. They measure it by split times and boat speed.

Investing should be measured the same way.

Trying harder does not improve results if effort is misapplied. Efficiency comes from understanding how markets work, how assets behave, and how time compounds small advantages.

In rowing terms, this is connection at the catch. A clean entry transfers power directly to the boat. Sloppy blade work wastes effort no matter how strong the rower is.

Financial fundamentals create that same connection.

Fundamentals Are the Foundation of Speed

Crews do not skip fundamentals to chase race pace. They build speed on top of balance, timing, and rhythm. Without those, speed collapses under pressure.

This section focuses on investing fundamentals for that reason.

How markets function.

Why volatility exists.

The difference between owning businesses and lending money.

How compounding builds momentum over time.

These are not advanced concepts. They are foundational ones. Ignoring them leads to emotional decisions and wasted motion.

Athletes who ignore technique plateau quickly. Investors who ignore fundamentals panic when conditions change.

Time Is the Course You're Racing On

Rowers do not fight the water. They learn to work with it.

Time plays that same role in investing. Markets move through cycles. Conditions shift. There are headwinds and tailwinds you cannot control. You control how long you stay in the race and how efficiently you move.

Speed in investing comes from staying invested long enough for compounding to work. That requires patience and restraint. It means trusting the stroke even when the boat does not surge immediately.

Trying to sprint a long race only guarantees fatigue.

Why Athletes Struggle With Financial Speed

Athletes are trained for intensity. Investing rewards endurance.

Athletes expect immediate feedback.

Markets delay feedback.

Athletes associate effort with results.

Markets reward discipline.

Athletes thrive under pressure.

Markets punish emotional reactions.

This mismatch causes frustration. Former athletes often feel like they should be doing more financially. More trading. More watching. More reacting. That instinct slows progress.

In rowing terms, it is rating up instead of lengthening the stroke.

The Right Kind of Speed

The chapters that follow focus on building sustainable speed.

Not by guessing.

Not by reacting.

Not by chasing.

But by understanding how markets work, how risk fits your long race plan, and how consistent execution compounds quietly over time.

Just like rowing, speed built on fundamentals lasts longer, holds up under pressure, and wins races that panic never could.

This is where you learn to move fast by staying smooth.

Chapter 9: How Financial Markets Really Work

Every rower remembers the first race where the boat felt out of control.

The start was fast.

The field surged.

Boats jumped ahead early.

The crowd got loud.

For a moment, it felt like panic was the only response. Rate up. Pull harder. Chase whatever shell was in front of you. Then, as the race unfolded, something became clear. The crews that stayed composed started to move. The ones that sprinted early began to fade. The water never changed. The difference was understanding.

Financial markets feel exactly the same to people who have not learned how they work.

From the outside, markets look chaotic. Prices move constantly. Headlines scream urgency. Opinions flood in from every direction. It feels like everyone else knows something you don't. That pressure pushes people to react instead of think.

Underneath that noise, markets are structured systems with rules, incentives, and patterns. Once you understand them, the chaos slows down. Just like rowing, the water doesn't calm. You do.

How Markets Function at the Most Basic Level

At their core, financial markets exist to move capital.

Some people and institutions need money.

Others have money they want to put to work.

Markets connect the two.

Companies raise capital to grow, hire, innovate, and compete. Governments borrow to fund infrastructure, defense, and public services. Investors supply that capital in exchange for ownership or repayment.

Prices do not move randomly. They move based on expectations. Not just about what is happening today, but about what people believe will happen in the future.

In rowing terms, the market is the course. Everyone races on the same water, but not everyone is racing the same race. Some are sprinting. Some are building endurance. Some are rebuilding entirely. The movement reflects competing strategies, not chaos.

The market is not designed to feel fair or calm.

It is designed to function.

Stocks, Bonds, and What Ownership Really Means

Many athletes invest without truly understanding what they own. That creates anxiety when prices move.

Stocks represent ownership.

When you buy a stock, you own a piece of a real business. That business sells products, pays employees, competes with rivals, and tries to make money. The stock price moves as expectations about that business change, but the business itself does not disappear because the price fluctuates.

In rowing terms, owning stock is being in the shell. You feel every surge and slowdown. Ownership means movement. It also means participation in long-term progress.

Bonds represent loans.

When you buy a bond, you are lending money to a company or government. In return, you receive interest and expect repayment at maturity.

In rowing terms, bonds are steady pressure at a controlled rate. Less volatile. Less exciting. Designed to provide stability and predictability.

Both play roles. You do not build a crew with only sprinters or only grinders. Balance matters.

Investing is not gambling.

It is owning and lending with intention.

Market Cycles and Volatility

Markets move in cycles.

Expansion.

Slowdown.

Correction.

Recovery.

This has always been true and always will be.

Volatility is not failure.

Volatility is movement.

Prices move because new information constantly enters the system. Earnings reports. Interest rate changes. Economic data. Global events. Expectations shift, and prices adjust.

In rowing terms, volatility is water conditions. Wind changes. Chop develops. Current shifts. None of that means the race is broken. It means crews must stay composed and execute fundamentals.

Athletes who panic during volatility make the same mistake as rowers who abandon technique when the water gets rough. They shorten strokes, rush the catch, and lose efficiency.

The market's job is not to feel smooth.

Its job is to reflect reality.

Why Early Leaders Rarely Decide the Race

Every regatta has boats that jump out early.

They sprint the first 500 meters.

They grab attention.

They make others feel behind.

Sometimes they win.

Often they fade.

Markets behave the same way. Certain stocks, sectors, or strategies lead for periods of time. Headlines follow them. Stories get written. Pressure builds to chase what is working right now.

That pressure causes mistakes.

Chasing early leaders ignores endurance, risk, and sustainability. Many investors abandon sound plans because they feel late to the race.

In rowing terms, this is rating up early and hoping fitness saves you later.

Sometimes it works.

Most of the time, it doesn't.

Long-Term Strategy vs Chasing Momentum

Long-term investing is about process, not prediction.

You do not need to know what will lead next.

You do not need to time every turn.

You do not need to react to every move.

You need a strategy that matches your time horizon, risk tolerance, and goals.

In rowing terms, this is race planning. You know your base pace. You know when to apply pressure. You know when to stay steady. You do not abandon the plan because another boat surges early.

Momentum feels powerful.

It is also temporary.

Discipline feels boring.

It is sustainable.

Markets reward the crews that stay in rhythm long after the noise fades.

Why Athletes Struggle With Financial Markets

Athletes are trained for immediate feedback.

You feel good reps.

You see progress.

You know when effort translates to results.

Markets delay feedback.

Good decisions can look bad short term.

Bad decisions can look good temporarily.

That disconnect frustrates athletes. It tempts them to change plans, force action, and chase reassurance. Over time, that behavior hurts outcomes.

In rowing terms, this is judging the race by the first ten strokes instead of the finish.

Coach's Perspective

What would your coach say?

Trust the plan.

Stay in rhythm.

Don't chase boats.

Control what you can control.

Finish strong.

No coach tells a crew to abandon strategy because another shell jumps ahead early. They reinforce fundamentals, composure, and discipline.

Markets reward the same mindset.

Game Situations and Decision Points

Situation One

Markets drop sharply.

Do you panic and exit, or do you recognize volatility as part of the race?

Financially, panic locks in mistakes.

Situation Two

A sector dominates headlines.

Do you chase momentum or evaluate whether it fits your long-term plan?

Financially, fit matters more than excitement.

Situation Three

You feel behind.

Do you increase risk recklessly or stay disciplined?

Financially, desperation destroys technique.

Each decision either preserves rhythm or breaks it.

Common Athlete Mistakes and Financial Parallels

Athletes chase early leads.

Financially, that leads to momentum chasing.

Athletes abandon technique under pressure.

Financially, that leads to emotional decisions.

Athletes confuse activity with progress.

Financially, that leads to overtrading.

Athletes forget endurance wins races.

Financially, that leads to short-term thinking.

Winning the Long Race

Financial markets reward ownership, patience, and discipline.

You do not need to lead every split.

You do not need to win every stretch.

You need to stay in the race long enough for the strategy to work.

Just like rowing, success comes from understanding the environment, respecting the process, and staying composed when others panic.

When you understand how markets really work, the chaos slows down. The noise fades. You stop reacting to every surge and start rowing your own race.

That is how long races are won.

Athlete Takeaways

- Markets move on expectations, not headlines
- Stocks mean ownership, bonds mean stability
- Volatility is movement, not failure
- Early leaders don't decide long races
- Discipline and rhythm beat panic every time

Chapter 10: Risk, Return, and the Power of Compounding

Every rower remembers the first time a coach talked about pace instead of power.

You wanted to pull harder.

You wanted to rate higher.

You wanted to prove you could handle more.

The coach slowed you down.

They talked about efficiency.

They talked about sustainability.

They talked about what happens over 2,000 meters, not the first 20 strokes.

That lesson shows up again and again in rowing. Speed is not about max effort at all times. It is about applying the right amount of pressure, at the right time, for the full length of the race.

Money works the same way.

Risk, return, and compounding are not complicated ideas. They are misunderstood because people approach them like short sprints instead of long rows. This chapter is about learning how to move faster over time by respecting risk, understanding volatility, and letting compounding do its job.

Risk and Reward Tradeoffs

There is no reward without risk.

Rowers understand this intuitively. You do not win races by rowing conservatively the entire time. You have to apply pressure. You have to take risks. But you also know that reckless moves flip boats.

In investing, higher potential returns come with higher risk.

Lower risk usually means lower expected returns.

There is no option that delivers high returns with no downside. Anyone promising that is either mistaken or dishonest.

In rowing terms, this is stroke pressure.

Light pressure is stable but slow.

Heavy pressure is faster but harder to sustain.

The goal is not to row every stroke at max power. The goal is to apply pressure in a way that matches your conditioning, your role in the boat, and the length of the race.

Financially, that means matching risk to:

- Your time horizon
- Your income stability
- Your flexibility
- Your goals

Risk is not something to avoid entirely.

It is something to manage intentionally.

Emotional Risk vs Financial Risk

Many athletes confuse discomfort with danger.

Seeing an account balance drop feels bad.

It creates anxiety.

It triggers doubt.

That is emotional risk.

Financial risk is different.

It is the risk of permanent damage.

The risk of losing money you cannot recover.

The risk of taking on exposure that does not match your situation.

In rowing terms, emotional risk is rowing in rough water. It feels unstable, but the shell is still sound. Financial risk is rowing with a cracked hull. One mistake ends everything.

Understanding this difference is critical.

Markets moving up and down is normal.

Volatility is expected.

It is not the same as failure.

Permanent loss usually comes from:

- Panic selling
- Overleveraging
- Chasing returns you do not understand
- Abandoning discipline under pressure

Athletes who mistake discomfort for danger make poor decisions at the worst times.

Volatility vs Permanent Loss

Volatility is movement.

Permanent loss is damage.

Markets move constantly. Prices rise and fall based on expectations, not just outcomes. That movement feels uncomfortable, especially if you are used to clear scoreboards and immediate feedback.

In rowing terms, volatility is chop and current.

Permanent loss is flipping the boat.

You cannot eliminate volatility.

You can eliminate many causes of permanent loss.

Staying diversified.

Avoiding leverage you do not control.

Matching investments to your time horizon.

Sticking with a plan through normal movement.

Missing a few strokes does not lose the race.

Jumping out of the boat does.

The Power of Compounding Over Time

Compounding is growth built on growth.

Your money earns returns.

Those returns earn returns.

Over time, the effect accelerates.

Early on, compounding feels slow.

Almost invisible.

That frustrates athletes who are used to seeing progress from hard work quickly. Compounding rewards patience, not intensity.

In rowing terms, this is base training.

One steady workout does not change much.

Weeks of consistent training build capacity.

Months and years change everything.

Compounding works the same way. The biggest gains often come later, not because you did anything different, but because time finally had enough space to work.

Time is the multiplier.

Not brilliance.

Not timing.

Time.

Why Starting Early Matters More Than Starting Big

Many athletes delay investing because they think small amounts do not matter.

"I'll start when I make more."

"I'll start later."

"I need to get settled first."

That logic costs more than most people realize.

Every year you delay is a year compounding cannot work for you. That time cannot be recovered.

In rowing terms, this is skipping base season. You can still race later, but you are always catching up.

You do not need to start big.

You need to start.

Consistency beats intensity.

Reps beat hero efforts.

Time beats timing.

The Hidden Cost of Waiting

Waiting feels safe.

It feels responsible.

It feels cautious.

It is often expensive.

People wait for:

- Better markets
- Higher income
- More certainty
- Perfect conditions

Those conditions rarely arrive.

Meanwhile, time keeps moving.

In rowing terms, this is sitting at the start line waiting for perfect water. The race happens anyway.

Starting imperfectly is better than waiting perfectly.

Why Athletes Often Over-Risk or Under-Risk

Athletes tend to swing between extremes.

Some over-risk.

They chase returns.

They want fast progress.

They assume confidence equals capacity.

Others under-risk.

They avoid discomfort.

They fear losses.

They keep everything safe and stagnant.

Both mistakes slow progress.

In rowing terms, one group sprints too early. The other never applies pressure. Neither wins long races.

The right approach is calibrated risk.

Pressure you can sustain.

Exposure that matches your conditioning.

Coach's Perspective

What would your coach say?

Trust your base.

Don't chase the sprint too early.

Stay within yourself.

Finish strong.

Consistency wins.

No coach tells a crew to empty the tank in the first 500 meters. They plan for the full race.

Your money deserves the same respect.

Game Situations and Decision Points

Situation One

Markets drop and your account is down.
Do you panic or recognize volatility as normal movement?
Financially, panic creates permanent loss.

Situation Two

You hear about high-return opportunities.
Do you chase or ask whether the risk fits your race?
Financially, mismatch causes damage.

Situation Three

You feel behind financially.
Do you force risk or recommit to consistency?
Financially, desperation ruins technique.
Each decision either supports compounding or interrupts it.

Common Athlete Mistakes and Financial Parallels

Athletes chase quick wins.
Financially, that leads to over-risking.
Athletes avoid discomfort.
Financially, that leads to stagnation.
Athletes skip base work.
Financially, that leads to delayed progress.
Athletes confuse effort with strategy.
Financially, that leads to poor outcomes.

Winning the Long Row

Compounding does not reward excitement.
It rewards consistency.
Risk is not the enemy.
Mismanaged risk is.

Volatility is not failure.

Permanent loss is.

The athletes who succeed financially are the ones who treat money like endurance sport. They stay patient. They stay disciplined. They trust the process even when results are slow.

That is how small decisions turn into meaningful outcomes.

Athlete Takeaways

- Risk and reward always move together
- Volatility is normal, permanent loss is avoidable
- Compounding rewards patience and repetition
- Waiting costs more than starting small
- Stay consistent, manage pressure, and finish strong

Chapter 11: Stocks Without the Sprint Mentality

Every rower learns this lesson the hard way.

There is always a crew that treats the race like a sprint. They explode off the line. High rate. Big power. The shell jumps early, and for a moment it looks impressive. The crowd notices. Other crews feel the pressure.

Then, somewhere before the halfway mark, the cost shows up.

Technique slips.

Breathing tightens.

The rate becomes frantic.

The boat loses run.

Rowing punishes sprint mentality over distance.

Stocks punish it too.

This chapter is about understanding stocks not as quick wins or hot tips, but as ownership in long-distance races. When you treat stocks like sprints, you burn out, panic, or crash. When you treat them like endurance investments, they quietly do their work.

What Owning Stock Actually Means

Buying a stock is not betting on a ticker.

It is not guessing price movement.

It is not chasing hype.

Buying a stock means owning a piece of a real business.

That business has employees, customers, competitors, costs, leadership, and strategy. It produces goods or services and tries to generate profit over time. Stock prices move daily, but businesses evolve slowly.

In rowing terms, owning stock is being in the shell, not watching from the launch.

You feel every surge and slowdown.

You sit through rough water.

You benefit when efficiency improves.

If you do not understand what the business does, how it makes money, or why it should exist long term, you are not investing. You are sprinting blind.

Ownership requires patience.

Ownership requires discipline.

Ownership requires staying seated when things get uncomfortable.

Why Athletes Struggle With Stocks

Athletes are trained to associate effort with immediate feedback.

You pull harder.

The boat responds.

You see splits change.

Stocks do not work that way.

You can make a good investment decision and see negative returns for months or even years. You can make a bad decision and get rewarded briefly. That disconnect tempts athletes to abandon discipline and chase reassurance.

In rowing terms, this is judging your training plan by one bad practice instead of the full season.

Stocks reward endurance thinking, not intensity.

Growth vs Value Investing

Two broad styles dominate stock investing.

Growth investing focuses on companies expected to expand quickly. These businesses often reinvest profits, trade at higher prices relative to current earnings, and experience more volatility. Expectations matter a lot.

Value investing focuses on companies priced lower relative to their fundamentals. These businesses may grow more slowly, but they often provide stability and resilience.

Neither style is right or wrong.

In rowing terms, growth stocks are high-rate crews pushing speed aggressively. Value stocks are long, powerful crews rowing efficiently at controlled rates.

Both can win races.

Problems arise when you expect one to behave like the other.

Growth will be volatile.

Value will be boring at times.

Smart investors respect roles instead of forcing everything to act the same way.

Dividends and Total Return

Dividends confuse many athletes.

Dividends are cash payments companies make to shareholders. They are not free money. They are part of how returns are delivered.

Total return includes:

- Price appreciation
- Dividends
- Reinvested earnings

Focusing only on dividends misses growth.

Focusing only on price ignores income.

In rowing terms, total return is boat speed, not just stroke rate or power. One metric never tells the whole story.

A steady crew rowing efficiently can beat a flashier crew that burns out. Dividends play that same stabilizing role in portfolios.

Why Sprint Mentality Fails in Stocks

Sprint mentality shows up as:

- Chasing hot stocks
- Overtrading
- Panicking during drawdowns
- Selling winners too early
- Holding losers too long hoping to get back to even

All of these behaviors come from impatience.

In rowing terms, this is rating up when the boat loses run instead of fixing technique.

Stocks are volatile.

Ownership requires tolerance for discomfort.

Progress happens unevenly.

Trying to force speed destroys efficiency.

Common Investing Myths Athletes Hear

Myth: Stocks are gambling

Reality: Ownership with discipline is investing. Guessing is gambling.

Myth: You have to pick winners

Reality: Consistency, diversification, and time matter more than precision.

Myth: Aggressive equals successful

Reality: Over-aggression creates mistakes.

Myth: You can time the market

Reality: Most people cannot, and repeated attempts usually reduce returns.

Rowing teaches respect for fundamentals. Stocks demand the same respect.

Long-Term Ownership Wins Races

The most successful stock investors are rarely the loudest. They do not brag about trades. They do not react to every headline. They focus on process.

They:

- Own businesses, not stories
- Stay invested through cycles
- Let compounding work
- Avoid unnecessary decisions

In rowing terms, they row their race.

They stay long.

They stay connected.

They finish strong.

Coach's Perspective

What would your coach say?

Lengthen the stroke.

Stay patient.

Don't chase other boats.

Trust your base.

Finish the race.

No coach encourages sprinting a 2,000-meter race. They build athletes to endure pressure and maintain technique.

Stocks demand the same discipline.

Game Situations and Decision Points

Situation One

A stock you own drops sharply.

Do you panic and sell, or reassess whether the business still fits your plan?

Emotion creates exits. Discipline creates opportunity.

Situation Two

You hear about a stock everyone is talking about.

Do you chase excitement or evaluate fundamentals?

Noise feels urgent. Fundamentals last.

Situation Three

Your portfolio feels boring.

Do you force action or respect that boredom often means discipline?

Boring is often efficient.

Common Athlete Mistakes and Financial Parallels

Athletes chase highlights.

Financially, that leads to hype investing.

Athletes abandon technique under pressure.

Financially, that leads to emotional selling.

Athletes confuse effort with effectiveness.

Financially, that leads to overtrading.

Athletes sprint races meant for endurance.

Financially, that leads to burnout.

Winning the Long Race

Stocks reward ownership, patience, and understanding.

You do not need to be perfect.

You do not need to be early.

You need to stay disciplined long enough for progress to show.

Just like rowing, success comes from staying connected when others panic and staying patient when others sprint.

That is how endurance wins.

Athlete Takeaways

- Stocks are ownership, not bets
- Growth and value play different roles in the boat
- Dividends are part of total return, not free money
- Sprint mentality destroys long-term efficiency
- Stay long, stay patient, and finish strong

Chapter 12: Bonds and Holding a Steady Rate

Every rower has felt the temptation to rate up when things feel uncertain.

The water gets choppy.

Another shell surges.

Your split ticks up.

Instinct says pull harder and raise the rate. Experienced rowers know better. There are moments when the fastest way forward is not more power. It is steadiness. Length. Control. Holding a rate you can sustain while others burn matches.

Bonds play that role in a portfolio.

They are not flashy. They do not dominate highlight reels. They rarely get credit when things are going well. But when conditions change, bonds help you hold your line, keep balance, and finish the race without blowing up.

This chapter is about understanding bonds for what they are and why steady pressure matters just as much as bursts of speed.

How Bonds Work

A bond is a loan.

When you buy a bond, you are lending money to a government or a company. In exchange, you receive interest payments and expect to get your original money back at maturity, assuming the borrower does not default.

That is it. No mystery.

Stocks give you ownership.

Bonds give you a contract.

In rowing terms, stocks are the power phase. Bonds are the recovery. You cannot row effectively without both. The recovery is not passive. It sets up the next stroke. Bonds do the same by providing income, stability, and predictability.

Bond prices can move, and that surprises people. Even though bonds are loans, their value changes as conditions change. Understanding why helps you use them correctly instead of fearing them.

Interest Rate Risk

Interest rates and bond prices move in opposite directions.

When interest rates rise, existing bonds with lower rates become less attractive. Their prices fall. When rates fall, existing bonds become more valuable. Their prices rise.

In rowing terms, this is current and wind. You do not control it, but you feel it. Fighting it wastes energy. Understanding it helps you adjust.

Interest rate risk matters more for longer-term bonds. Shorter-term bonds feel rate changes less. This is why bond maturity matters when building a portfolio.

Rising rates do not mean bonds are broken. They mean conditions changed. Bonds still do their job over time by paying interest and returning principal.

Credit Risk

Credit risk is the risk that the borrower cannot repay the loan.

Governments with strong economies tend to have lower credit risk. Companies with stable cash flow tend to have lower credit risk. Higher yields often signal higher risk.

In rowing terms, credit risk is boat integrity. You want a shell you can trust under pressure. You might row an older shell if conditions are calm. You do not want to race rough water in something fragile.

Higher yields can be tempting. Just like rating up can feel powerful. Both increase risk. Understanding what you are lending to matters more than the promised return.

When Bonds Make Sense

Bonds are not about maximizing returns. They are about controlling outcomes.

Bonds tend to make more sense when:

- You need money in the near to intermediate future
- You value income and stability
- Your responsibilities increase
- You want to reduce portfolio swings
- You want dry powder to rebalance during volatility

In rowing terms, this is knowing when to settle the rate.

Young crews with long races ahead can afford to push. Crews protecting a lead or managing fatigue rely on rhythm and control. Neither approach is better. They are situational.

Bonds are tools. Not trophies.

Stability in a Diversified Portfolio

Bonds provide balance.

They often move differently than stocks, especially during stress. That difference matters more than average returns. Stability allows you to stay invested when emotions run high.

In rowing terms, bonds are balance in the shell. You do not notice them when things are smooth. You feel their absence immediately when something goes wrong.

A diversified portfolio needs:

- Assets that grow
- Assets that stabilize
- Assets that provide flexibility

Ignoring bonds entirely is like rowing with everyone trying to sprint. It feels aggressive until it falls apart.

Why Athletes Undervalue Bonds

Athletes are conditioned to chase performance.

Speed.

Power.

Output.

Bonds feel boring. They do not excite. They do not make headlines. That makes them easy to dismiss.

But rowing teaches that boring is often efficient.

Long races are won by crews who stay composed while others chase surges. Bonds help portfolios do the same.

Bonds do not exist to make you rich quickly. They exist to keep you from making mistakes that derail progress.

How Bonds Support Discipline

One of the biggest benefits of bonds is behavioral.

When markets drop, portfolios with bonds tend to feel less extreme. That reduces panic. It reduces the urge to sell at the wrong time. It allows you to rebalance instead of react.

In rowing terms, bonds keep the shell set when conditions deteriorate. They give you something to lean on.

Discipline is easier when the boat feels stable.

Coach's Perspective

What would your coach say?

Hold the rate.

Stay long.

Don't chase.

Protect the shell.

Finish the piece.

No coach tells a crew to sprint the entire race. They teach pacing, patience, and control. Bonds bring that same mindset into investing.

Game Situations and Decision Points

Situation One

Markets become volatile.

Do you abandon your plan or lean on stability?

Financially, stability keeps you in the race.

Situation Two

You need money in a few years.

Do you chase returns or protect capital?

Financially, timing matters.

Situation Three

Your portfolio feels slow.

Do you remove defense or respect balance?

Financially, imbalance creates mistakes.

Each decision reflects whether you value endurance or excitement.

Common Athlete Mistakes and Financial Parallels

Athletes undervalue recovery.

Financially, that means ignoring bonds.

Athletes chase speed constantly.

Financially, that means too much risk.

Athletes ignore conditions.
Financially, that means poor timing.
Athletes confuse boredom with inefficiency.
Financially, that leads to unnecessary changes.

Winning the Long Race

You do not win long races by sprinting the whole way.

You win by holding a sustainable rate, protecting technique, and staying composed when others fall apart.

Bonds do not steal speed.

They preserve it.

They slow the game down.

They reduce mistakes.

They give you options.

That is how endurance wins.

Athlete Takeaways

- Bonds are loans designed to provide stability
- Interest rate and credit risk explain bond movement
- Bonds matter more as timelines shorten and stakes rise
- Stability helps you stay disciplined under pressure
- Holding a steady rate wins long races

Chapter 13: Funds, ETFs, and Crew-Based Investing

Every rower eventually learns that great boats do not rely on one person doing everything.

Even the strongest athlete cannot carry a shell alone. Speed comes from coordination. Timing. Trust. When each seat does its job and moves together, efficiency rises and mistakes drop. When someone tries to hero the race, the boat suffers.

Funds and ETFs work the same way.

They are crew-based investing. Instead of relying on one stock, one company, or one idea to carry your future, you spread the workload across many participants. That structure reduces risk, increases consistency, and allows you to stay in the race through long seasons.

This chapter is about understanding how funds and ETFs work, why they matter, and how to use them without overcomplicating your plan.

Opening Story From the Sport

Think about a lineup decision before a big regatta.

You could stack the boat with the strongest erg scores and hope raw power wins. Or you could seat athletes who move well together, match timing, and trust the rhythm. Every experienced coach chooses the second option.

Raw strength matters.

Synchronization matters more.

Investing is no different. Individual stocks can be powerful. But building everything around a few names creates fragility. Funds and ETFs create coordination across hundreds or thousands of investments, allowing the portfolio to move smoothly even when one seat struggles.

Mutual Funds vs ETFs

Both mutual funds and exchange-traded funds pool money from many investors and invest it across a diversified group of assets. The main difference is how they trade and how flexible they are.

Mutual funds are typically priced once per day. You buy or sell at the end-of-day price. They are often used in retirement plans and long-term strategies.

ETFs trade throughout the day like stocks. Prices move as the market moves. They offer flexibility and transparency.

In rowing terms, both run organized systems.

Mutual funds are steady, controlled training rows.

ETFs are race-ready shells that respond immediately.

Neither is inherently better. What matters is the strategy inside the fund, not the wrapper around it.

Index Strategies vs Active Strategies

Index investing aims to match the performance of a specific market. It is rules-based, consistent, and low cost. Index funds do not try to outsmart the market. They aim to capture it.

Active investing tries to outperform the market through selection and timing. Managers make decisions about what to own, what to avoid, and when to adjust.

In rowing terms, index investing is running a proven race plan. Active investing is trusting individual playmaking and tactical adjustments.

Both can work.

Both can fail.

The risk comes from assuming active strategies will consistently deliver better results without understanding how difficult that is. Most athletes benefit from building around a core index-based system and using active strategies carefully, if at all.

Crew boats win more races than solo efforts.

Fees and Expense Ratios

Fees matter more than most people realize.

Expense ratios reduce returns every year, regardless of performance. They compound against you quietly. One percent does not feel like much in a single year. Over decades, it is massive.

In rowing terms, fees are like drag.

You might not notice it at first.

Over distance, it changes everything.

Low-cost funds do not guarantee success. High-cost funds make success harder. Paying more does not mean you are getting more skill. It often means you are subsidizing complexity.

Efficiency matters.

Diversification Without Complexity

Diversification is not about owning everything.

It is about spreading risk intelligently.

Different companies.

Different sectors.

Different regions.

Different roles.

Funds and ETFs make this simple. One decision can give you exposure to hundreds or thousands of investments. That reduces the impact of any single failure.

In rowing terms, this is roster balance. You do not need eight stars. You need eight athletes who fit together and execute their roles.

Complexity does not equal sophistication.

Simplicity does not equal laziness.

The best crews keep the system clean and repeatable.

Why Athletes Often Resist Funds

Athletes are conditioned to believe individual talent wins.

You train to stand out.

You compete for seats.

You chase personal performance.

That mindset carries into investing. Picking stocks feels like skill. Funds feel passive. That perception causes athletes to underestimate how hard consistent outperformance really is.

In rowing terms, this is confusing flash with speed.

Crew-based investing does not remove skill. It removes unnecessary pressure. It lets the system do the work while you stay disciplined.

When Funds and ETFs Shine

Funds and ETFs are especially powerful when:

- You want consistency
- You want diversification without constant decisions
- You want to reduce emotional mistakes
- You want to focus on long-term progress

They reduce the need to react. They reduce the temptation to chase noise. They keep the shell moving even when one seat struggles.

That is not weakness.

That is strategy.

Coach's Perspective

What would your coach say?

Trust the system.

Move together.

Do your job.

No hero strokes.

Finish as a crew.

No coach builds a race plan around one athlete improvising. They build systems that hold up under pressure.

Funds and ETFs allow you to invest the same way.

Game Situations and Decision Points

Situation One

You want simplicity.

Do you build diversified exposure or chase individual names?

Financially, simplicity often protects discipline.

Situation Two

You hear about a high-fee product with bold promises.

Do you evaluate cost and role or get distracted by marketing?

Financially, drag compounds.

Situation Three

You want consistency.

Do you trust a system or force action for excitement?

Financially, boredom often means efficiency.

Common Athlete Mistakes and Financial Parallels

Athletes rely on individual talent.

Financially, that means concentrated risk.

Athletes ignore efficiency.

Financially, that means high fees.

Athletes complicate execution.

Financially, that leads to confusion and mistakes.

Athletes chase highlights.

Financially, that leads to unnecessary risk.

Winning the Long Race

Crew boats win long races because they move together.

Funds and ETFs allow you to invest with coordination, discipline, and balance. They reduce the need for constant decisions and help you stay invested when emotions rise.

This is not about avoiding responsibility.

It is about building a system that holds up under pressure.

That is how championships are built.

Quietly.

Consistently.

Together.

Athlete Takeaways

- Funds and ETFs spread the workload across a crew
- Index strategies provide consistency and efficiency
- Active strategies require skill and restraint
- Fees act like drag over long distances
- Crew-based investing keeps you moving when others panic

Chapter 14: Real Estate and Alternative Courses

Every rower eventually learns that not every race is won by staying in the middle of the course.

Sometimes conditions favor the inside line.

Sometimes the outside water is cleaner.

Sometimes switching lanes too early costs more than it gains.

The best crews understand options. They know when to stay the course and when to take an alternative line. They also know that changing course adds complexity, risk, and responsibility. You do not switch lanes just because it looks interesting. You do it because it fits the conditions and your capabilities.

Real estate and alternative investments are those alternative courses.

They can be powerful.

They can add strength.

They can also slow you down or flip the boat if you do not understand the trade-offs.

This chapter is about knowing when these courses make sense, when they do not, and how to approach them without losing rhythm.

Renting vs Owning: Choosing the Right Line

Renting and owning are not identities.

They are tools.

Athletes often feel pressure to own as a symbol of progress. That pressure ignores context. In rowing terms, that is switching lanes because another crew did, not because it fits your race.

Renting offers:

- Flexibility
- Lower upfront costs
- Easier exits
- Fewer unexpected responsibilities

Owning offers:

- Stability
- Potential appreciation
- Forced savings through mortgage payments
- Control over the space

Neither is better in every situation.

In rowing terms, renting is staying light in the shell. You can adjust quickly. You can move when conditions change. Owning is committing to a longer, heavier line. It can be powerful if conditions are right, but it limits quick moves.

Buying too early can restrict mobility, career options, and cash flow. Renting too long can delay progress when stability is already in place. The correct decision depends on income stability, time horizon, location, and lifestyle.

Progress is not defined by ownership.

It is defined by fit.

Real Estate as an Investment Is Not Just a House

Many athletes confuse living in real estate with investing in real estate.

Owning a home is first a lifestyle decision.

It may become an investment over time.

That is not guaranteed.

Real estate investing introduces additional variables:

- Location risk
- Maintenance
- Property taxes
- Insurance
- Vacancy
- Financing terms

In rowing terms, this is adding weight to the shell. If the crew is strong and coordinated, the boat still moves. If not, drag increases quickly.

Real estate can generate income and appreciation. It can also demand time, capital, and emotional energy. That trade-off matters.

REITs and Indirect Ownership

You do not have to be a landlord to invest in real estate.

Real Estate Investment Trusts allow investors to own pieces of income-producing properties through publicly traded vehicles. REITs can provide exposure to commercial buildings, apartments, warehouses, healthcare facilities, and more.

In rowing terms, REITs are off-seat contributions. You are still part of the boat's movement without handling every oar.

REITs offer:

- Liquidity
- Diversification

- Professional management
- Easier access than direct ownership

They also come with:

- Market volatility
- Interest rate sensitivity
- Less control than direct ownership

REITs can be a smart way to gain real estate exposure while keeping flexibility and simplicity. They are not perfect. They are tools.

Alternatives: More Than Just a Different Stroke

Alternative investments include assets outside traditional stocks and bonds.

Common examples include:

- Commodities
- Private equity
- Private credit
- Hedge strategies
- Tangible assets

These investments are often marketed as diversifiers or return enhancers. Sometimes they are. Often they come with trade-offs that are underappreciated.

In rowing terms, alternatives are specialty strokes. They have specific uses. They are not substitutes for fundamentals.

Alternatives often involve:

- Higher fees
- Less transparency
- Longer lockups

- Complex structures

Complexity does not equal advantage.

It equals responsibility.

Before adding alternatives, you need a strong base. Balance. Liquidity. Discipline. Without those, alternatives amplify mistakes instead of reducing risk.

Liquidity: Staying Able to Adjust

Liquidity is how easily you can access your money.

Stocks and bonds are generally liquid.

Real estate and many alternatives are not.

That difference matters more than people expect.

Illiquid investments limit flexibility. If cash is needed unexpectedly, you may be forced to sell at the wrong time or take on debt. Illiquidity is not inherently bad, but it must be intentional.

In rowing terms, liquidity is maneuverability. When conditions change, crews that can adjust lanes and rate survive. Crews locked into one option struggle.

Liquidity creates options.

Options create calm.

Calm supports discipline.

Risk Shows Up Differently Outside Traditional Markets

Risk in real estate and alternatives is not always obvious.

It can show up as:

- Inability to sell
- Unexpected expenses
- Capital calls
- Regulatory changes

- Concentration in one asset or location

In rowing terms, this is hidden drag. The boat feels fine until pressure increases, then problems surface.

These risks do not mean alternatives should be avoided. They mean they should be respected. Understanding where risk hides is part of rowing smart water.

Why Athletes Are Drawn to Alternatives

Athletes are comfortable with complexity.

They trust hard things.

They believe effort and intelligence create advantage.

That mindset makes alternatives appealing.

Private deals feel exclusive.

Real estate feels tangible.

Commodities feel strategic.

Sometimes those instincts are right.

Often they create overconfidence.

In rowing terms, this is assuming a new stroke will be faster without mastering timing first.

Alternatives reward patience, capital, and understanding. They punish urgency and ego.

When Real Estate and Alternatives Make Sense

These courses tend to fit best when:

- Core fundamentals are already strong
- Cash flow is stable
- Liquidity needs are met
- Time horizon is long
- Complexity is manageable

They are not shortcuts.

They are extensions.

Used well, they add power.

Used early or poorly, they restrict movement.

Coach's Perspective

What would your coach say?

Know the water.

Choose your line carefully.

Don't change course without reason.

Protect the shell.

Finish the race you're in.

No coach praises unnecessary complexity. They reward smart decisions that preserve speed and balance.

Game Situations and Decision Points

Situation One

You feel pressure to buy property.

Do you evaluate fit or chase status?

Financially, status decisions create drag.

Situation Two

You hear about a private investment.

Do you understand liquidity and risk or just projected returns?

Financially, projections don't row the boat.

Situation Three

You want diversification.

Do you add complexity before fundamentals are solid?

Financially, sequencing matters.

Each decision either adds strength or reduces flexibility.

Common Athlete Mistakes and Financial Parallels

Athletes chase harder courses too early.

Financially, that means illiquid investments before readiness.

Athletes confuse difficulty with effectiveness.

Financially, that means overcomplication.

Athletes underestimate recovery and flexibility.

Financially, that means ignoring liquidity risk.

Athletes follow others without context.

Financially, that leads to poor fit.

Winning the Long Race

Real estate and alternatives can be powerful additions.

They are not required.

They are not trophies.

They are tools.

Long races are won by crews who choose lines intentionally, respect conditions, and protect their ability to adjust. Financial success works the same way.

Stay balanced.

Stay liquid enough to adapt.

Add complexity only when it serves the plan.

That is how you take alternative courses without losing rhythm.

Athlete Takeaways

- Renting and owning are tools, not identities
- Real estate adds responsibility along with opportunity
- REITs offer exposure without hands-on management
- Alternatives increase complexity and reduce liquidity
- Choose courses intentionally and protect your ability to adjust

Part IV: Mid-Race Adjustments (Managing the Portfolio)

Every crew knows that races are not run in a straight line from start to finish.

There's the start, where adrenaline spikes and tension is high.

There's the middle, where rhythm matters more than raw effort.

And there's the finish, where discipline pays off.

In the middle of the race—when the field spreads out and conditions shift—the crews that win are not the ones who panic or abandon their plan. They are the ones who adjust without losing rhythm. They stay connected, maintain timing, and correct small errors before they become big ones.

Managing your investment portfolio is the same.

The race does not end once you invest. Markets move. Life changes. Your goals evolve. Staying invested without a plan for adjustment is like rowing without paying attention to the water: it feels fine until momentum disappears.

This section—**Mid-Race Adjustments**—is about understanding how to manage your portfolio so that it stays aligned with your goals, risk tolerance, and life changes, without overreacting to every wave in the water.

What "Managing the Portfolio" Really Means

In rowing, once the race is underway, every adjustment is intentional.

You do not fix a small wiggle by slamming the rudder.

You correct technique.

You adjust pressure.

You stay synchronized.

Managing the portfolio works the same way.

It is not a daily reaction to headlines.

It is thoughtful alignment with your long-term plan.

Part of this involves:

- Reviewing your investments on a schedule
- Making adjustments when your mix drifts too far
- Incorporating life changes
- Avoiding emotional over-trading

The guiding idea is discipline over reaction, rhythm over panic.

Portfolio Drift and Why It Happens

Your target mix of assets—your allocation between stocks, bonds, and cash—is like your race strategy. It reflects how much risk you can handle and how long your race (time horizon) is.

But markets do not move evenly.

If stocks outperform bonds over several years, your stock allocation grows larger as a percentage of your total holdings. That moves your portfolio away from where it started and where your plan expects it to be. If this goes unchecked, your risk tolerance may be unintentionally higher than you chose.

Adjusting back to your plan is called **rebalancing**. It helps maintain your target asset mix so your portfolio stays in sync with your risk tolerance and goals.

In rowing terms, rebalancing is like making tiny course corrections. You are not steering wildly based on wind gusts. You are returning to the rhythm that produces steady speed.

How Often to Review and Adjust

Checking the lineup every stroke is noise.

Checking only at the finish is risk.

Experts often recommend scheduled check-ins—like quarterly or semi-annual reviews—to make sure your strategy still fits your goals and risk tolerance.

These check-ins are not about reacting to every move in the market. They are about ensuring that:

- Your asset allocation still matches your intended plan
- Your investments still serve the role you assigned them
- Nothing in your life (job change, income shift, new responsibilities) requires a strategic update

Scheduled reviews prevent small issues from becoming big ones.

Rebalancing: Trimming the Leaders, Boosting the Laggards

When stocks grow faster than bonds, they start to take up a bigger share of your portfolio than planned. Rebalancing literally means trimming what has grown and adding to what has fallen behind to bring the mix back in line.

That process does three things:

1. Maintains your intended risk profile
2. Keeps your investment strategy disciplined
3. Enforces a buy-low, sell-high habit without emotion

In rowing, this is like rotating seat pressure so each athlete contributes efficiently and the shell moves smoothly. You are not abandoning the strategy because one seat got ahead. You are keeping the system balanced.

Life Changes and Portfolio Updates

Life events matter.

Getting married.

Buying a home.

Changing careers.

Starting a family.

Each of these changes your timeline and how much risk you can afford. The portfolio you had five years ago may not fit the life you have today.

Adjustments are not admissions of failure. They are professionalism.

Just as a coach adapts a plan when a new athlete joins the crew, your portfolio should evolve when your life changes.

Avoiding Over-Coaching

Too much adjustment creates confusion.

One of the biggest mistakes investors make is **ACTION** without alignment—trading frequently, chasing performance, or changing strategy every time the market gets noisy.

Over-coaching in rowing ruins rhythm.

Over-trading in investing destroys efficiency.

Discipline is not inactivity.

It is knowing when action is necessary and when patience is better.

Coach's Perspective

What would your coach say?

Make smart corrections.

Do not overreact.

Trust the process.

Stay in your stroke.

Adjust when necessary, not when anxious.

A coach would never tell a crew to change strategy because another boat surged. They would reinforce fundamentals and correct errors quietly.

Investing works the same way.

Game Situations and Decision Points

Markets swing sharply.

Do you rebalance or panic?

Life changes.

Do you update your goals or ignore reality?

You're restless.

Do you act or stay disciplined?

The right adjustment is often the calm one.

Common Athlete Mistakes and Financial Parallels

Athletes tighten up under pressure.

Financially, that means over-trading.

Athletes ignore feedback.

Financially, that leads to outdated strategies.

Athletes confuse motion with improvement.

Financially, that creates noise and costs.

Winning the Long Race

Mid-race adjustments do not mean fixing everything that moves. They mean staying in rhythm while making smart, intentional corrections.

Rebalancing keeps you aligned.

Portfolio updates keep you relevant.

Discipline keeps you steady.

Winning crews adjust without losing rhythm.
Winning investors do the same.

Chapter 15: Asset Allocation and Seat Balance

Every experienced rower knows this truth.

You can have strong athletes in every seat and still lose the race if the boat is not balanced.

Seat assignments matter. Stroke rate matters. Power application matters. If one side pulls harder, the shell wobbles. If one seat rushes, timing breaks down. Speed does not come from one athlete overpowering the rest. It comes from balance, rhythm, and alignment.

Asset allocation is your financial seat balance.

It determines how power is applied across your portfolio, how stable the shell feels in rough water, and how well you can maintain speed over long distances. Get allocation right, and the boat runs smooth. Get it wrong, and even good investments start working against each other.

This chapter is not about picking the best investment. It is about placing each asset in the right seat so the whole system works.

Stocks, Bonds, and Cash: Assigning the Seats

Every portfolio is built on three core asset classes.

Stocks

Bonds

Cash

Each has a role. None should dominate the boat.

Stocks are your power seats. They drive long-term growth. They respond to conditions, surge when the water is right, and fade when conditions turn rough. Stocks are volatile, but over long races, they generate most of the speed.

Bonds are your stabilizers. They dampen movement, absorb shock, and keep the shell from getting too jumpy when conditions change. Bonds rarely win races on their own, but they prevent disasters.

Cash is your balance point. It does not generate speed, but it provides flexibility. It allows you to respond to unexpected conditions without disrupting the boat. Cash is how you make adjustments without panic.

In rowing terms:

- Stocks are raw power
- Bonds are control and stability
- Cash is maneuverability

Too much power without control flips the boat.

Too much control without power stalls progress.

Too much idle weight creates drag.

Balance is everything.

Domestic vs International Exposure: Rowing Beyond One Course

Some crews only ever train on one stretch of water.

Same conditions. Same currents. Same patterns.

That works until race day brings unfamiliar conditions.

Limiting your investments to one country is similar. The global economy includes different growth cycles, demographics, industries, and risks. While markets are connected, they do not move in perfect sync.

International exposure broadens your race environment.

In rowing terms, this is training on different water, in different wind, against different competition. You become less dependent on one course behaving perfectly.

Global diversification does not eliminate volatility. It spreads it.

When one region struggles, another may recover faster or behave differently. That does not guarantee better returns every year. It reduces the chance that one economic environment controls your entire outcome.

This is not about predicting which country wins.

It is about avoiding overdependence on one course.

What Diversification Really Means in a Boat

Diversification is one of the most misunderstood concepts in investing.

It does not mean owning everything.

It does not mean complexity.

It does not mean adding seats until the boat is crowded.

Diversification means spreading risk intelligently.

Different assets respond differently to inflation, interest rates, growth, and stress. When combined thoughtfully, they smooth the ride and reduce the impact of any single failure.

In rowing terms, diversification is proper crew balance.

You do not stack all your strongest athletes on one side and hope the other side keeps up. You distribute strength so timing stays intact.

Concentration creates fragility.

Diversification creates durability.

That durability matters most when conditions deteriorate. Calm water hides flaws. Rough water exposes them.

Career-Stage Allocation: Adjusting the Boat Over Time

No crew rows the same way at every stage of the race.

Early on, the focus is acceleration and positioning.

Mid-race, efficiency and rhythm matter most.

Late in the race, control and execution decide outcomes.

Your asset allocation should evolve the same way.

Early in your career, time is your biggest asset. You can tolerate more volatility because recovery time is long. Growth assets often dominate the boat. The focus is building speed, not protecting position.

As income grows and responsibilities increase, balance shifts. Mortgages, families, career risk, and lifestyle stability change how much volatility you can handle. Bonds and cash start playing larger roles.

Later, as timelines shorten, protection and reliability matter more than raw growth. The race becomes about finishing strong, not sprinting early.

In rowing terms:

- Young crews pull harder
- Experienced crews pull smarter

Neither is better. They are situational.

The mistake is freezing allocation at one stage and refusing to adapt. Asset allocation is not static. It should change as your life changes.

Why Asset Allocation Matters More Than Investment Selection

Many investors obsess over picking winners.

The best stock.

The hottest fund.

The next opportunity.

That mindset misses the bigger picture.

A great athlete in the wrong seat disrupts the boat.

An average athlete in the right seat improves speed.

Asset allocation drives most long-term results because it controls:

- Risk exposure
- Volatility
- Behavior under stress
- Sustainability across seasons

Selection matters, but structure matters more.

A poorly allocated portfolio forces emotional decisions. A well-allocated portfolio allows discipline to survive rough water.

Coach's Perspective

What would your coach say?

Balance the boat.

Stay in sync.

Do your job.

Trust the setup.

Row your seat.

Coaches do not redesign the shell every race. They focus on alignment, rhythm, and discipline. They know speed comes from the system, not hero pulls.

Game Situations and Decision Points

Your portfolio grows faster than expected.

Do you rebalance or let risk creep higher?

Life changes.

Do you adjust allocation or ignore reality?

Markets get volatile.

Do you trust the setup or abandon it?

The right seat balance makes these decisions easier.

Common Athlete Mistakes and Financial Parallels

Athletes overpower the stroke.

Financially, that shows up as overconcentration.

Athletes ignore balance.

Financially, that shows up as poor diversification.

Athletes refuse to adjust race strategy.

Financially, that leads to outdated allocation.

These mistakes do not show up immediately.

They show up when conditions get tough.

Winning the Long Race

Asset allocation is not about predicting markets.

It is about preparing for different conditions.

When the boat is balanced, you can apply power confidently. When it is not, every stroke feels forced.

Get seat balance right, and everything else works better.

Ignore it, and no amount of effort fixes the wobble.

Athlete Takeaways

- Speed comes from balance, not brute force
- Stocks, bonds, and cash each have a seat for a reason
- Diversification keeps the shell stable in rough water
- Allocation should evolve as your race and life evolve
- A balanced boat lets you row hard without flipping

Chapter 16: Buying, Holding, and Trusting the Stroke

Every rower has felt this moment.

The start is clean. The boat jumps. The first few strokes feel powerful. Then the urge hits. Pull harder. Rush the slide. Add rate before the shell is ready. It feels productive in the moment, but timing breaks, efficiency drops, and the boat slows.

Great crews learn to trust the stroke.

They commit to rhythm. They believe the setup will carry them. They know that speed comes from consistency, not panic. Investing works the same way. Buying, holding, and trusting the process matters far more than reacting to every splash around you.

This chapter is about execution. Not strategy. Not theory. Execution under pressure.

Opening and Funding Accounts: Getting the Boat in the Water

You cannot race if the boat is still on the rack.

Opening investment accounts is not exciting, but it is essential. Brokerage accounts, retirement accounts, and savings vehicles are simply tools. They do not make you fast. They allow you to participate.

Many athletes delay investing because they feel unprepared. They want to know more. They want perfect timing. They want certainty. That hesitation costs more than small mistakes ever will.

In rowing terms, this is standing on the dock waiting for ideal water while other crews are already training.

Funding accounts matters just as much as opening them. Money sitting in checking is like athletes sitting on the bench. Potential exists, but nothing happens until they are in the race.

Automatic contributions matter here. Just like daily practices build fitness, regular funding builds progress. Consistency beats intensity every time.

You do not need a perfect setup.

You need to start rowing.

Market Orders vs Limit Orders: Stroke Timing Matters

How you enter the market affects efficiency, but not in the way most people think.

Market orders execute immediately at the current price. They prioritize participation over precision. Limit orders specify a price and wait until the market meets it.

In rowing terms, this is timing the catch.

A market order is committing to the stroke when the blade is ready. A limit order is waiting for ideal placement. Both have uses. Problems arise when waiting becomes avoidance.

Most long-term investors benefit from simplicity. Over time, entry price matters far less than time in the water. Missing months or years waiting for the perfect entry does far more damage than slightly imperfect execution.

Precision feels smart.

Participation creates results.

The market rewards those who keep rowing, not those who stand still waiting for perfect conditions.

Buy-and-Hold Discipline: Settling Into Rhythm

Buy-and-hold investing is not passive.

It is disciplined.

It means committing to a strategy and letting time do the work. It means understanding that markets move, cycles repeat, and volatility is normal. It means resisting the urge to change stroke every time conditions shift.

In rowing terms, buy-and-hold is maintaining rate through chop.

You do not abandon the stroke because the water gets rough. You clean it up. You stay connected. You trust the setup.

Athletes struggle with buy-and-hold because they are wired to react. In sports, adjustments are constant. In investing, too many adjustments create drag.

Buy-and-hold does not mean ignoring your portfolio.

It means avoiding unnecessary changes.

Reviews matter. Rebalancing matters. Panic does not.

The market will test your patience. It always does. Those who survive are not the smartest. They are the most consistent.

Avoiding Emotional Decisions: Staying in the Boat

Emotions flip boats faster than mistakes.

Fear shows up when markets drop. Greed shows up when markets surge. Confidence turns into overconfidence when things go well for too long.

In rowing terms, this is abandoning technique under pressure.

When the crowd gets loud or competitors surge, inexperienced crews rush. They shorten strokes. They lose length. They stop trusting the stroke.

Experienced crews stay calm. They trust the rhythm. They let others make mistakes.

Financially, emotional decisions usually show up as:

- Selling after losses
- Chasing recent winners

- Changing strategy mid-race
- Overtrading

These actions feel protective. They are destructive.

The goal is not to eliminate emotion.

The goal is to prevent emotion from driving decisions.

Systems help here. Automatic investing. Predefined allocation. Scheduled reviews. These are your rigging and foot stretchers. They hold you in position when pressure rises.

The Difference Between Activity and Progress

Athletes love activity.

Reps feel productive.

Sweat feels earned.

Investing punishes unnecessary activity.

Checking accounts daily.

Tweaking allocations weekly.

Jumping between strategies.

Responding to headlines.

This creates the illusion of control without improving outcomes.

In rowing terms, this is overworking the slide without moving the boat faster.

Progress comes from:

- Staying invested
- Keeping rhythm
- Applying power consistently
- Avoiding self-inflicted mistakes

Less activity often produces better results.

Coach's Perspective

What would your coach say?

Trust the stroke.

Stay in rhythm.

Do not rush the slide.

Let the boat run.

One stroke at a time.

Coaches know that panic destroys technique. They also know that the crews who win are not the ones who look frantic. They look calm.

Execution beats emotion.

Game Situations and Decision Points

Markets drop sharply.

Do you sell to feel safe or keep rowing?

Markets surge.

Do you chase or stay disciplined?

You feel bored.

Do you tinker or trust the plan?

These moments decide outcomes more than market returns.

Common Athlete Mistakes and Financial Parallels

Athletes rush the catch.

Financially, that shows up as bad timing decisions.

Athletes change stroke under pressure.

Financially, that shows up as strategy abandonment.

Athletes confuse effort with speed.

Financially, that shows up as overtrading.

The boat does not care how hard you pull if timing is broken.

Winning the Long Race

Buying and holding is not about stubbornness.

It is about discipline.

Markets reward those who stay invested through uncertainty. The biggest gains often happen after the hardest periods to stay calm.

You do not win long races by sprinting constantly.

You win by trusting the stroke when others panic.

Athlete Takeaways

- Get the boat in the water before worrying about perfect conditions
- Participation matters more than precision over long races
- Buy-and-hold is discipline, not passivity
- Emotion flips boats faster than bad markets
- Trust the stroke and let time create speed

Chapter 17: Rebalancing and Rate Changes

Every rower knows this feeling.

The boat is moving well. The rhythm is solid. Then, slowly, almost unnoticed, things drift. One side starts pulling a little harder. The rate creeps up. Timing slips just enough to feel off, but not enough to force an immediate correction. If nobody adjusts, the shell loses balance and speed fades.

Great crews fix this early.

They do not panic. They do not tear everything apart. They make small, intentional adjustments to bring the boat back into sync. That is exactly what rebalancing does in your financial life.

Rebalancing is not a reaction to failure. It is maintenance. It is how you keep efficiency over a long race.

How Often to Review Investments: Checking the Set, Not Staring at the Water

You do not stare at the bow ball every stroke.

In rowing, constant checking kills rhythm. But ignoring the boat entirely allows problems to grow. The same is true with investing.

Most investors benefit from scheduled reviews, not constant monitoring. Annual or semiannual reviews are usually enough to stay aligned. The purpose is awareness, not micromanagement.

In rowing terms, this is checking the set during steady-state work. You feel the boat. You make mental notes. You adjust calmly.

Checking investments daily increases anxiety without improving outcomes. Markets move constantly. Most of that movement is noise. Reacting to every splash leads to rushed decisions and broken rhythm.

The goal of a review is simple:

Are you still rowing the race you intended to row?

Rebalancing Strategies: Bringing the Boat Back to Level

Rebalancing means restoring balance.

Over time, different assets grow at different speeds. Stocks may surge while bonds lag. Cash may shrink relative to the rest of the portfolio. Without adjustment, your original plan quietly changes.

Rebalancing trims what has grown too large and adds to what has fallen behind. It feels counterintuitive because it often means selling what feels good and buying what feels uncomfortable.

In rowing terms, this is correcting pressure.

If one side starts overpowering the boat, speed does not improve. It suffers. Rebalancing restores symmetry so power transfers cleanly into forward motion.

There are a few common approaches:

- Calendar-based rebalancing, such as once per year
- Threshold-based rebalancing, when allocations drift beyond set ranges
- Contribution-based rebalancing, using new money to restore balance

The exact method matters less than consistency. What hurts performance is ignoring imbalance until it becomes extreme.

Rebalancing enforces discipline when emotion would otherwise take over.

Life Changes and Portfolio Updates: When the Course Changes

Not all adjustments are market-driven.

Life changes matter more than headlines.

New job.

Marriage.

Children.

Buying a home.

Career shifts.

Health changes.

Each of these alters timelines, responsibilities, and risk capacity. Ignoring them is like rowing the same race plan after the course changes.

In rowing terms, this is wind and current awareness.

If conditions shift, crews adjust rate and pressure. They do not pretend the water stayed the same.

Your portfolio should evolve as your life evolves. What made sense at twenty-five may not make sense at forty-five. Growth-heavy strategies often shift toward stability as responsibilities increase and timelines shorten.

Adjustment is not weakness.

It is professionalism.

Avoiding Over-Correction: Don't Chase Every Ripple

Over-correction ruins boats.

A small timing issue turns into chaos when rowers overreact. Stroke rate jumps. Technique falls apart. The shell slows dramatically.

Investing has the same risk.

Too many changes create friction. Overtrading increases costs and taxes. Constant strategy shifts destroy consistency. Emotional responses replace planning.

In rowing terms, this is changing stroke every time the water gets choppy.

Sometimes the best adjustment is restraint. Trusting what is already working. Letting the boat run.

Discipline is not inactivity.

It is selective action.

If your plan is sound and aligned with your life, most market movements require patience, not response.

Rebalancing vs Market Timing

Rebalancing is not market timing.

Market timing tries to predict where markets are going. Rebalancing responds to where your portfolio has drifted. One is speculative. The other is structural.

In rowing terms, market timing is guessing when the other crew will sprint. Rebalancing is keeping your own rhythm intact.

You do not need to predict the next move.

You need to stay aligned with your plan.

The Emotional Benefit of Rebalancing

Rebalancing is not just mechanical. It is psychological.

It gives you permission to act calmly. It replaces fear and greed with rules. It creates confidence during uncertainty.

When markets fall, rebalancing reminds you that volatility was expected. When markets surge, it prevents overconfidence from rewriting your plan.

In rowing terms, this is confidence in training.

Crews that trust their preparation do not panic mid-race. They rely on habits built long before the pressure arrived.

Coach's Perspective

What would your coach say?

Stay balanced.

Make small corrections.

Do not overreact.

Trust your base.

Finish the race you trained for.

Coaches know that most races are lost by panic, not effort. The same is true financially.

Game Situations and Decision Points

Markets move sharply.

Do you rebalance or panic?

Your income changes.

Do you adjust your plan or ignore reality?

You feel uneasy.

Do you trust structure or chase comfort?

These moments separate disciplined investors from emotional ones.

Common Athlete Mistakes and Financial Parallels

Athletes over-adjust mid-race.

Financially, that shows up as overtrading.

Athletes ignore small imbalances.

Financially, that shows up as unmanaged risk drift.

Athletes confuse motion with speed.

Financially, that shows up as constant tinkering.

Balance wins long races.

Winning the Long Race

Rebalancing is not exciting.

It is effective.

It keeps your plan aligned. It manages risk quietly. It allows you to stay invested when others fall apart.

Long races are not won by dramatic moves.

They are won by crews who stay balanced stroke after stroke.

Athlete Takeaways

- Check the boat on a schedule, not every stroke
- Rebalancing restores rhythm without panic
- Life changes matter more than market noise
- Over-correction kills efficiency
- Small, calm adjustments win long races

Chapter 18: The Mental Side of Money

Every rower remembers racing in rough water.

The wind picks up. The chop gets unpredictable. Boats around you surge and stall. The rate feels harder to hold. Your legs burn, your lungs scream, and the temptation to panic creeps in. The crews that fall apart are rarely the weakest physically. They are the ones that lose composure.

Money works the same way.

Most financial outcomes are not determined by intelligence, access, or even opportunity. They are determined by behavior under pressure. The mental side of money is what separates athletes who build long-term stability from those who repeatedly sabotage themselves despite doing many things right.

Pressure, Patience, and the Long Pull

Rowing is built on patience.

You do not win races by sprinting the first five hundred meters. You win by holding rhythm, conserving energy, and trusting that disciplined pressure applied over time will separate you from the field. Impatient crews burn out early. Patient crews finish strong.

Investing demands the same mindset.

Pressure shows up when markets drop. Accounts decline. Headlines turn negative. Doubt creeps in. The urge to do something, anything, feels overwhelming.

Patience is the ability to stay seated, keep your hands steady, and trust the stroke you committed to before the race started.

Financially, patience means understanding that short-term discomfort is part of long-term progress. Markets do not reward perfect timing. They reward endurance.

The long pull matters more than the first burst.

Comparison: Racing Your Own Lane

In rowing, you cannot see the entire field clearly.

You catch glimpses of other boats. You hear crowds reacting. You sense movement in your peripheral vision. But if you turn your head too much, the boat suffers.

Comparison in money works the same way.

Friends buy homes.

Co-workers talk about hot investments.

Social media shows curated success.

Comparison creates urgency that does not belong to you. It pushes you to speed up when your plan does not require it. It encourages decisions that fit someone else's race.

In rowing terms, this is abandoning your lane to chase another shell.

The most dangerous comparison is not performance. It is timing. Someone else's success might be built on a completely different starting point, income level, or risk profile. Trying to match outcomes without matching context leads to mistakes.

You are not racing them.

You are racing the distance.

Crowd Noise and Outside Influence

Every race has noise.

Spectators shout.

Coaches yell splits.

Other crews surge unexpectedly.

Noise is not information. It is stimulus.

Financial markets generate constant noise. Headlines. Predictions. Opinions. "Experts" who were confident yesterday and wrong today. The louder the noise, the more emotional the environment becomes.

In rowing terms, this is racing past the grandstands.

Crews that react to every shout lose rhythm. Crews that stay locked in move cleanly through the chaos.

Noise feels urgent. Discipline feels boring. The boring approach wins.

Learning to filter information is a skill. Not every opinion deserves attention. Not every market movement requires action.

Staying composed means limiting what you consume and choosing sources intentionally. Less input often leads to better decisions.

Building Systems for Discipline

Mental toughness is not about willpower.

Rowers do not rely on motivation mid-race. They rely on training. Reps. Muscle memory. Systems that work when fatigue sets in.

Money requires the same approach.

Systems protect you when emotions spike.

Automatic contributions.

Diversified portfolios.

Scheduled reviews.

Clear rules for when action is allowed.

These systems remove decision-making during moments of stress. They act like a coxswain calling rhythm when the crew is exhausted.

If your financial success depends on how you feel in the moment, you will eventually fail. Feelings are unreliable in rough water.

Systems create consistency even when confidence wavers.

Staying Composed in Rough Water

Rough water is unavoidable.

Markets drop.

Interest rates change.

Jobs shift.

Life surprises you.

Composure does not mean ignoring reality. It means responding deliberately instead of reacting emotionally.

In rowing, rough water demands technique, not panic. You shorten the slide slightly. You stay connected through the finish. You protect the set of the boat.

Financially, this means:

Not checking balances constantly.

Not changing strategy mid-storm.

Not confusing volatility with failure.

Rough water exposes preparation. Crews that trained well handle it. Crews that relied on calm conditions fall apart.

The same is true with money.

The Hidden Cost of Emotional Decisions

Emotional decisions rarely feel reckless in the moment.

They feel justified.

Protective.

Urgent.

Selling after losses feels responsible.

Chasing gains feels smart.

Waiting feels safe.

The damage shows up later.

Missed recoveries.

Higher taxes.

Lost compounding.

Permanent setbacks.

In rowing terms, this is losing the race by inches after blowing rhythm early.

Most financial mistakes are not dramatic. They are small decisions made repeatedly under stress.

Coach's Perspective

What would your coach say?

Control what you can control.

Stay in your lane.

Trust the stroke.

Next ten.

Do not flinch.

Coaches know that mental discipline wins races long before the finish line.

Game Situations and Decision Points

Markets drop quickly.

Do you abandon rhythm or stay seated?

You hear about someone else's gains.

Do you chase or refocus?

Uncertainty rises.

Do you tighten up or trust your preparation?

These moments define outcomes.

Common Athlete Mistakes and Financial Parallels

Athletes race others instead of the course.

Financially, that leads to comparison-driven decisions.

Athletes panic in rough water.

Financially, that leads to selling low.

Athletes rely on emotion instead of training.

Financially, that leads to inconsistency.

Winning the Long Race

The mental side of money determines whether discipline survives pressure.

Those who stay composed, filter noise, and rely on systems outperform those who chase feelings. The goal is not to eliminate emotion. It is to prevent emotion from running the race.

Long races reward calm crews.

Long financial journeys do the same.

Athlete Takeaways

- Pressure reveals preparation, not talent
- Comparison pulls you out of your lane
- Noise is not the same as information
- Systems beat willpower in rough water
- Composure wins long races

Part V: The Long Pull and Life After Competition

Every rower understands the long pull.

It is not the start, when adrenaline carries the boat.

It is not the final sprint, when the line is in sight.

It is the long stretch in between, where the rhythm settles, fatigue builds, and the work becomes quiet and repetitive. The boat is moving, but nothing feels dramatic. This is where races are actually won.

Life after competition feels like this phase.

The uniform comes off. The season ends. The structure that once dictated your days disappears. There is no race circled on the calendar. No coach calling splits. No obvious finish line ahead. What remains is endurance, self-discipline, and the ability to keep pulling with purpose when no one is watching.

This part of the book is about that stretch.

When Motivation Stops Being Obvious

During competition, motivation is clear.

You train because there is a race.

You endure discomfort because the payoff is visible.

You know when to push and when to recover.

After sports, that clarity fades.

Financial goals stretch years or decades into the future. Career progress is uneven. Life responsibilities stack gradually. Feedback slows down. Many former athletes mistake this phase for stagnation when it is actually a different kind of race.

In rowing terms, this is steady state.

The stroke rate drops.

The effort is controlled.

The gains are subtle but real.

Trying to sprint through this phase leads to burnout. Learning to hold pressure without panic is what creates long-term progress.

The Shift From External Structure to Internal Control

One of the biggest adjustments after sports is structural.

In competition, discipline is enforced. Practice times are set. Training plans are handed to you. Accountability is external. After sports, all of that disappears. No one tells you when to save, invest, rest, or push. You become responsible for your own structure.

In rowing terms, you become your own coxswain.

That freedom feels good at first. It also carries risk. Without structure, drift sets in. Small lapses compound. The long pull exposes whether discipline was learned or borrowed.

This part of the book focuses on building structure that lasts without whistles, schedules, or pressure from above.

Redefining Progress Without a Scoreboard

Athletes are used to measurable progress.

Splits.

Seats.

Placements.

Wins.

Life after sports removes the scoreboard. Progress becomes harder to see, which makes comparison tempting. Income, titles, houses, and lifestyle start to replace performance as markers of success.

The long pull requires a different definition of winning.

Progress looks like stability.

It looks like options.

It looks like flexibility under pressure.

It looks like peace of mind.

These wins do not show up on highlight reels, but they determine quality of life.

Endurance Over Excitement

The topics in this section are not flashy.

Taxes.

Retirement planning.

Career development.

Housing decisions.

Family conversations.

Estate planning.

Choosing advisors.

Avoiding costly mistakes.

None of these feel urgent day to day. All of them matter enormously over time.

In rowing terms, these are technical details that preserve efficiency. Small leaks that go unaddressed eventually slow the boat. Clean execution keeps momentum steady.

The long pull rewards attention to fundamentals long after excitement fades.

Why Former Athletes Are Built for This Phase

Former athletes often underestimate their advantage.

You understand delayed gratification.

You know how to train without immediate results.

You respect systems, reps, and consistency.

You have endured long seasons where effort preceded reward.

The long pull rewards exactly those traits.

The difference now is choice. Discipline is no longer mandatory. Structure must be intentional. Progress depends on habits you maintain privately.

Those who embrace this phase build durable lives. Those who resist it feel restless, stuck, or burned out.

Carrying Momentum Without Burning Out

The long pull is not about grinding endlessly.

Rowers know how to apply pressure without maxing out every stroke. Sustainable pace preserves form. Life after sports works the same way.

You do not need constant intensity.

You do not need to optimize everything.

You do not need to win every comparison.

You need rhythm.

You need direction.

You need enough pressure to keep moving forward.

This part of the book is about staying in the boat for decades, not chasing short bursts of validation.

The Quiet Stretch That Decides Everything

The crowd is gone.

The noise is lower.

The work is steady.

This is where outcomes are decided.

Life after competition is not an afterthought. It is the main race. Those who learn to value endurance, patience, and quiet discipline build lives that feel stable, flexible, and aligned.

The pull is longer now.

The rhythm matters more.

The rewards run deeper.
Keep rowing.

Chapter 19: Taxes and Where You Apply Power

Every rower learns this early.

You can pull as hard as you want, but if you apply power at the wrong time or in the wrong direction, the boat slows down. Good rowing is not about raw effort. It is about *where* and *how* force is applied. Clean catches, connected finishes, and efficient sequencing turn strength into speed. Sloppy power just creates splash.

Taxes work the same way.

It is not only about how much you earn or invest. It is about how much of that effort actually moves you forward. Taxes determine whether your financial power transfers cleanly into progress or leaks away quietly over time.

This chapter is about learning where to apply power so your effort counts.

Taxable vs Tax-Advantaged Accounts: Different Water, Different Resistance

Not all water rows the same.

Flat water rewards long, clean strokes. Choppy water punishes inefficiency. You adjust technique based on conditions.

Financially, taxable and tax-advantaged accounts are different water.

Taxable accounts give you flexibility. You can invest, sell, and access money at any time. The tradeoff is friction. Interest, dividends, and capital gains are taxed along the way. Every stroke meets resistance.

Tax-advantaged accounts are designed for efficiency over distance. Retirement accounts, health savings accounts, and similar vehicles allow growth to be taxed differently, often later or not at all.

In rowing terms, taxable accounts are rowing into a headwind. You can still move the boat, but it takes more effort. Tax-advantaged accounts are protected water. Same stroke. More glide.

The mistake many athletes make is ignoring account type and focusing only on investments. Where you row matters just as much as how hard you pull.

Tax-Deferred vs Tax-Free Growth: Choosing When the Resistance Shows Up

Tax-deferred growth means you delay taxes until later. Contributions may reduce taxes now, but withdrawals are taxed in the future. Tax-free growth means you pay taxes upfront and future withdrawals are not taxed.

Neither is automatically better.

The question is timing.

In rowing terms, this is choosing how to distribute effort across the race. Do you push harder early and conserve later, or hold back early and finish strong? The right answer depends on the course, the conditions, and your role in the boat.

If your income is high now and likely lower later, deferring taxes can make sense. If your income is lower now and likely higher later, paying taxes upfront for tax-free growth can be powerful.

The mistake is defaulting to convenience instead of strategy. Smart crews do not guess. They plan.

Asset Location Basics: Putting the Right Rowers in the Right Seats

Asset location is about *where* you hold investments, not *what* you hold.

Some investments generate frequent taxable income. Others are more tax-efficient. Holding them in the wrong account creates unnecessary drag.

In rowing terms, this is seat placement.

You do not put your strongest rower in a seat where timing matters most if they cannot hold rhythm. You do not waste technical skill where brute force is needed. You place athletes where their strengths translate best.

Financially, that means:

- Higher-turnover or income-heavy investments often belong in tax-advantaged accounts
- More tax-efficient investments often belong in taxable accounts
- Cash belongs where it remains accessible

Asset location does not change your stroke rate.

It changes how far each stroke carries the boat.

This is one of the most overlooked efficiency gains in personal finance.

Common Tax Mistakes That Bleed Speed

Most tax mistakes are not dramatic. They are slow leaks.

Ignoring taxes entirely and hoping it works out

Using only one type of account because it feels simpler

Making decisions based on headlines instead of personal context

Waiting until filing season to think about strategy

Selling investments without understanding tax consequences

In rowing terms, these are technical flaws that cost length every stroke. You still move forward, but you fall behind crews that row cleaner.

Taxes punish reaction and reward planning. The earlier you think about them, the easier they are to manage.

Taxes and Behavior: Why Planning Beats Panic

Taxes influence behavior more than people admit.

Fear of taxes can keep people from investing.

Fear of taxes can cause people to hold poor investments too long.

Fear of taxes can delay smart decisions.

In rowing terms, this is shortening the stroke because you are afraid of catching a crab. Playing scared limits speed.

The goal is not to eliminate taxes. The goal is to understand them well enough that they stop controlling your decisions. When taxes are planned for, they lose their emotional power.

Coach's Perspective

What would your coach say?

Apply power cleanly.

Do not waste strokes.

Be efficient, not frantic.

Row the water you are in.

Details matter over distance.

Coaches know that races are lost through inefficiency long before they are lost through effort.

Game Situations and Decision Points

You earn more income.

Do you adjust where you save, or keep rowing inefficient water?

You invest in something new.

Do you consider taxes, or hope it works out later?

It is late in the year.

Do you plan calmly, or scramble reactively?

Clean application of power wins long races.

Common Athlete Mistakes and Financial Parallels

Athletes pull harder instead of cleaner.

Financially, that means earning more while leaking efficiency.

Athletes ignore technique under fatigue.

Financially, that means ignoring taxes until damage is done.

Athletes react late.

Financially, that means missed planning opportunities.

Winning the Long Race

You cannot avoid taxes.

You can control how much drag they create.

Applying power in the right place allows the same effort to go farther. Over decades, that difference compounds quietly and dramatically.

The crews that win long races are not the ones who panic about resistance. They adjust technique and keep moving.

Athlete Takeaways

- Not all water rows the same. Account type matters
- Tax-deferred and tax-free growth are pacing decisions
- Asset location is seat placement for your money
- Small tax leaks cost speed over long distances
- Clean power application beats harder pulling

Chapter 20: Retirement Accounts and Financial Independence

Every rower understands training for a race that is far away.

You put in meters months before race day. You lift for strength you will not test immediately. You row steady state knowing the payoff is later, not today. The work feels repetitive. Sometimes boring. Always necessary. The freedom you feel on race day comes from preparation you barely remember doing.

Retirement planning works the same way.

Financial independence is not about a specific age. It is about control. It is the ability to decide how you spend your time without being forced by money. Retirement accounts exist to help you build that freedom slowly, deliberately, and efficiently over the longest race of your life.

Employer Plans and Pensions: Free Speed You Don't Ignore

For many athletes, the first real opportunity to invest consistently comes through an employer plan.

401(k)s, 403(b)s, and similar plans allow you to save automatically from each paycheck. That automation matters. It removes decision-making and builds rhythm. Many employers also offer matching contributions.

That match is not a bonus.

It is compensation.

In rowing terms, an employer match is flat water with a tailwind. You do not row past it. You take advantage of it.

Pensions, when available, function differently. They promise future income based on years of service and salary. They reduce uncertainty but often require long-term commitment to one organization.

Both systems reward consistency. Missing out because you planned to “start later” is like skipping winter training and hoping spring work fixes everything.

Traditional and Roth IRAs: Choosing When You Pay the Cost

IRAs give you options beyond employer plans.

Traditional IRAs allow tax-deferred growth. Contributions may reduce taxes today, but withdrawals are taxed later. Roth IRAs work in reverse. You pay taxes now, and qualified withdrawals later are tax-free.

Neither option is universally better.

The question is timing.

In rowing terms, this is pacing strategy.

Do you apply more pressure early and protect energy later, or conserve early and finish strong? The right choice depends on your current income, expected future income, and long-term goals.

Many athletes benefit from using both over time. This creates flexibility later when tax conditions are uncertain. You are not betting on one perfect answer. You are building optionality.

Contribution Rules: Respecting the Course Markers

Retirement accounts come with rules.

Contribution limits.

Income restrictions.

Required distributions.

Penalties for early withdrawals.

These rules are not punishments. They are structure.

In rowing terms, this is the course layout. Buoys exist to keep races fair and efficient. Ignoring them leads to penalties or disqualification.

Understanding contribution limits helps you prioritize where each dollar goes. Exceeding limits creates unnecessary problems. Missing opportunities wastes distance you can never recover.

The most important rule is consistency. You do not need perfect timing. You need regular strokes.

Withdrawal Rules: Finishing Without Crashing

Saving for retirement is only half the race.

The other half is how you use it.

Withdrawal rules determine when and how money can be accessed without penalties. Early withdrawals often trigger taxes and penalties that permanently reduce what your money can do for you.

In rowing terms, this is the final thousand.

You do not sprint blindly. You protect form. You finish strong without falling apart.

Retirement income planning focuses on sustainability. How long does the money need to last? How are taxes managed? How does spending adjust over time?

The goal is not to empty the account as fast as possible. The goal is to keep the boat moving smoothly for the entire remaining distance.

Financial Independence: What the Finish Line Really Looks Like

Financial independence is often misunderstood.

It is not quitting work.

It is not unlimited spending.

It is not never worrying again.

It is choice.

Choice to work less.

Choice to work differently.

Choice to say no to situations that do not align with your life.

In rowing terms, financial independence is rowing because you want to, not because someone is forcing you to.

Retirement accounts are tools that create that choice. They are not exciting. They are powerful because they work quietly while you live your life.

Why Athletes Struggle With Retirement Planning Early

Many athletes delay retirement saving because the payoff feels too far away.

The mistake is thinking retirement is a destination instead of a process.

Compounding rewards time, not intensity. Early contributions matter more than large contributions later. Waiting feels safe. It is expensive.

In rowing terms, this is skipping base work and relying on late sprints. It rarely works.

Starting imperfectly beats starting late.

Coach's Perspective

What would your coach say?

Start now.

Take the free speed.

Trust the process.

Row your meters.

Finish what you start.

Coaches know that championships are built in the offseason. Financial independence is no different.

Game Situations and Decision Points

Your employer offers a match.

Do you take it or leave speed on the water?

You qualify for an IRA.

Do you use it or delay because it feels complicated?

You want flexibility later.

Do you plan now or hope it works out?

The long race rewards early discipline.

Common Athlete Mistakes and Financial Parallels

Athletes skip base work.

Financially, that means delaying retirement savings.

Athletes focus only on power.

Financially, that means ignoring tax efficiency.

Athletes underestimate distance.

Financially, that means running out of options later.

Winning the Long Race

Retirement accounts do not win races today.

They win freedom later.

They reward consistency, patience, and respect for structure. When used correctly, they turn small, steady strokes into meaningful independence.

You do not need to be perfect.

You need to stay in the boat.

Athlete Takeaways

- Retirement accounts are long-distance training, not race-day tactics
- Employer matches are free speed you do not pass up
- Traditional and Roth accounts are pacing tools, not guesses
- Rules exist to protect long-term performance
- Consistent strokes build financial independence

Chapter 21: Housing and Major Financial Decisions

Every rower recognizes the moment when a race slows down.

The boat is moving, but conditions change. Wind shifts. The course tightens. This is not the time to rush. It is the time to settle, check balance, and make clean decisions. Crews that panic waste energy. Crews that stay composed keep momentum.

Major financial decisions work the same way.

Buying a home. Financing a car. Signing a long lease. Making purchases that lock in years of payments. These moments do not happen often, but when they do, they shape everything that follows. They deserve patience, clarity, and awareness, not emotion.

Renting vs Buying: Tools, Not Identity

Renting and buying are not moral choices.

They are tools.

Renting offers flexibility. Lower upfront costs. Easier exits. Fewer surprises. It is often the right move early in a career, during transitions, or when mobility matters.

Buying offers stability. Potential appreciation. Forced savings through mortgage payments. It can make sense when income is steady, timelines are long, and you plan to stay put.

In rowing terms, renting is staying light and adaptable. Buying is setting the boat and committing to a long, steady course. Neither is better in every situation.

The mistake many former athletes make is treating buying as a marker of success instead of a strategic decision. Purchasing a home before income, location, or lifestyle has stabilized can restrict options and increase stress.

Progress is not defined by ownership.

It is defined by fit.

Mortgages and Down Payments: Committing to the Course

A mortgage is long-term debt attached to a physical asset.

The monthly payment matters.

The interest rate matters.

The down payment matters.

But so does everything else.

Property taxes.

Insurance.

Maintenance.

Repairs.

Time and energy.

In rowing terms, this is committing to a long piece at a fixed rate. You need conditioning, recovery, and depth to sustain it. If income is unstable or flexibility matters, heavy commitments can slow you down.

A larger down payment reduces pressure and increases margin for error. A smaller down payment preserves cash but increases leverage and risk. There is no universal rule. The right choice depends on your stability, savings, and tolerance for uncertainty.

What matters most is not qualifying for a mortgage, but sustaining it comfortably.

Cars, Leases, and Financing Traps

Cars are one of the most common financial leaks.

They depreciate.

They feel necessary.

They are easy to finance.

Monthly payments make expensive decisions feel manageable, especially when income is rising. Over time, those payments pile up with everything else.

Leases can offer lower payments but limit flexibility and often lead to repeat cycles of obligation. Long loans reduce payments but increase total cost and keep you underwater longer.

In rowing terms, this is overrating flash at the expense of efficiency.

Transportation is a tool. It should support your life, not define it. Reliable, boring choices preserve flexibility and reduce stress. Expensive upgrades feel good briefly and cost you every month.

Cars do not make you faster.

They weigh the boat down.

Planning Major Purchases: Seeing the Whole Course

Big purchases deserve planning.

That means understanding the full cost, not just the payment. It means knowing how a decision affects cash flow, savings, investing, and flexibility.

If one purchase forces you to:

Drain emergency savings

Pause retirement contributions

Increase anxiety

Reduce options

It is too big.

In rowing terms, this is stroke selection under fatigue. You do not force power if it compromises balance. You choose the stroke that keeps the boat moving cleanly.

Major decisions should fit within your financial rhythm, not disrupt it.

Emotional Pressure and Status Decisions

Major purchases often come with pressure.

Peers buying homes.

Social media showcasing upgrades.

Cultural expectations about success.

Pressure creates urgency that does not belong to you.

In rowing terms, this is sprinting because another crew surges, even when it does not fit your race plan.

Status-driven decisions feel justified in the moment and expensive over time. They trade long-term flexibility for short-term validation.

You do not need to win every comparison.

You need to stay in your lane.

Flexibility Is an Asset

Flexibility does not show up on balance sheets.

It shows up in options.

Ability to change jobs.

Ability to relocate.

Ability to handle surprises.

Ability to say no.

Every large fixed commitment reduces flexibility. That does not make it wrong. It makes it something to evaluate carefully.

In rowing terms, flexibility is boat balance. You feel it when conditions change.

Smart financial decisions preserve room to adjust.

Coach's Perspective

What would your coach say?

Slow it down.

Know the course.

Make the simple play.

Do not force it.

Protect your rhythm.

Big moments require composure, not ego.

Game Situations and Decision Points

You feel pressure to buy.

Do you evaluate fit or chase status?

You qualify for financing.

Do you ask whether you should take it or just whether you can?

You want something now.

Do you consider long-term impact or short-term relief?

The moment passes.

The decision stays.

Common Athlete Mistakes and Financial Parallels

Athletes rush big moments.

Financially, that leads to overcommitment.

Athletes play to the crowd.

Financially, that leads to expensive status purchases.

Athletes underestimate recovery.

Financially, that leads to stress and regret.

Winning the Long Race

Housing and major purchases should support your life, not restrict it.

The smartest decisions usually feel calm, not urgent. They preserve flexibility, protect cash flow, and allow you to keep rowing steadily through changing conditions.

You do not win long races by forcing power.

You win by staying balanced and committed to the full distance.

Athlete Takeaways

- Renting and buying are tools, not identities
- Mortgages and car payments commit future strokes
- Monthly payments hide long-term drag
- Flexibility is a competitive advantage
- Big decisions deserve patience, not pressure

Chapter 22: Your Career Is Your Longest Race

Every rower knows that no single piece defines a season.

You can win an early race and still miss the podium at the championship. You can struggle early and still peak when it matters. What separates great rowers from talented ones is not one result. It is how they train, adapt, and endure over time.

Your career works the same way.

Investments matter. Saving matters. Planning matters. But nothing drives your long-term financial outcome more than your ability to earn, grow, and adapt across decades. Your career is your longest race. It sets the pace for everything else.

Treating it casually is like neglecting conditioning and hoping technique alone carries you through a six-thousand-meter season.

Salary vs Total Compensation: Looking Beyond the Split Time

Salary is the number everyone talks about.

It is clean. Easy to compare. Highly visible. But salary alone tells an incomplete story.

Total compensation includes:

Bonuses and incentives

Retirement plan contributions and matches

Health insurance and benefits

Paid time off

Flexibility and remote options

Professional development

Long-term growth opportunities

In rowing terms, salary is split time. Total compensation is boat speed.

You can pull a fast split and still lose ground if timing, balance, and efficiency are off. Two jobs with the same salary can produce very different financial outcomes depending on benefits, stability, and growth potential.

Former athletes often focus too heavily on salary because it feels like the scoreboard. Professionals learn to evaluate the full race.

Job Changes and Benefits: Every Move Resets the Course

Changing jobs is like changing boats.

New rigging.

New lineup.

New expectations.

Benefits reset with every move. Health insurance changes. Retirement plans change. Vesting schedules reset. Paid time off accrual starts over. These details matter more than most people realize.

In rowing terms, this is learning a new shell. Even if you are strong, performance suffers until you understand the setup.

Job changes can accelerate growth when planned well. They can also introduce instability if made impulsively. Chasing small salary increases without understanding benefit tradeoffs often costs more than it gains.

Before changing roles, ask:

What am I gaining?

What am I giving up?

How does this affect my long-term rhythm?

The goal is not constant movement. It is intentional progression.

Negotiation Basics: Applying Pressure Without Rushing

Negotiation makes many former athletes uncomfortable.

It feels confrontational.

It feels awkward.

It feels like asking for something you did not earn.

That mindset is wrong.

Negotiation is communication. It is clarity about value, expectations, and alignment. Athletes negotiate all the time without realizing it. Playing time. Roles. Leadership opportunities. Trust.

In rowing terms, negotiation is pressure control.

You do not yank the oar.

You connect cleanly.

You apply force at the right moment.

Preparation matters. Know your contributions. Understand market context. Be clear about what you want and why. Silence and patience are often more powerful than aggressive demands.

Small improvements compound. A slightly higher salary, better benefits, or more flexibility early in a career echoes for decades.

Side Income and Entrepreneurship: Expanding Your Stroke Set

Side income attracts athletes because it feels like opportunity.

Coaching.

Consulting.

Content creation.

Business ownership.

Investments tied to personal brand or skills.

Side income can increase flexibility and resilience. It can also create distraction, burnout, and complexity if poorly structured.

In rowing terms, this is expanding your stroke set.

Adding a strong mid-race move makes you harder to beat. Flailing without structure slows the boat.

Side income should support your main career, not undermine it. Taxes, time management, legal structure, and risk matter. Not every opportunity deserves a yes.

The question is not can you do it.

The question is should you do it now.

Career Risk Is Financial Risk

Many athletes underestimate career risk.

Injuries end seasons.

Markets fluctuate.

Industries change.

Roles disappear.

Your career is not guaranteed. Skills matter. Relationships matter. Adaptability matters.

In rowing terms, this is cross-training.

Crews that rely on one strength struggle when conditions change. Athletes who continue developing skills stay competitive longer.

Career development is a form of financial protection. The more adaptable and valuable you are, the more control you have over income and choices.

Burnout and the Trap of Overpulling

Former athletes often overwork.

They replace training schedules with long hours. They push without recovery. They confuse grind with progress.

In rowing terms, this is rowing every piece at race pace.

It feels productive.

It is not sustainable.

Careers are marathons disguised as sprints. Burnout kills earning power just as effectively as bad decisions. Recovery, boundaries, and pacing matter.

The goal is longevity, not constant strain.

Coach's Perspective

What would your coach say?

Develop your engine.

Know your role.

Communicate clearly.

Apply pressure with purpose.

Play the long game.

Coaches understand that talent gets you in the boat, but habits keep you there.

Game Situations and Decision Points

You receive an offer.

Do you evaluate total compensation or chase salary alone?

You feel underpaid.

Do you prepare and negotiate, or stay silent and resentful?

You see a side opportunity.

Do you assess impact and risk, or chase excitement?

Career decisions echo for years.

Common Athlete Mistakes and Financial Parallels

Athletes rely on talent alone.

Financially, that means neglecting skill development.

Athletes avoid uncomfortable conversations.

Financially, that leaves money and opportunity on the table.

Athletes overtrain.

Financially, that leads to burnout and stalled growth.

Winning the Long Race

Careers are built deliberately.

They reward consistency, adaptability, and self-awareness. When your earning power is developed and protected, every other part of your financial life becomes easier to manage.

You do not need to win every sprint.

You need to stay competitive across seasons.

Your career is your longest race.

Train for it accordingly.

Athlete Takeaways

- Salary is a split, not the whole race
- Total compensation determines real speed
- Job changes reset benefits and risk
- Negotiation is clean pressure, not conflict
- Sustainable careers beat short bursts of grind

Chapter 23: Estate Planning Basics Everyone Needs

Estate planning sounds distant to most athletes.

It feels like something for later. For older people. For families with more money, more time, more complexity. That assumption causes more damage than almost any other delay in personal finance.

Estate planning is not about death. It is about control.

Rowers understand this instinctively. You do not wait until the final hundred meters to decide who sets the rhythm, who steers, and who calls the move. Those decisions are made long before the race starts so that, under pressure, no one is guessing.

Estate planning does the same thing for life.

It ensures the right people make decisions, at the right time, with clarity, not confusion.

Wills and Trusts: Installing the System Before Race Day

A will is the most basic form of estate planning.

It outlines who receives your assets, who handles your affairs, and who makes decisions for minor children if applicable. Without a will, the state steps in and applies default rules that are slow, expensive, and impersonal.

In rowing terms, a will is a basic race plan.

It is not fancy, but it prevents chaos. Everyone knows their role. The boat has direction.

A trust is a more advanced tool. Trusts allow for greater control over how and when assets are distributed. They can reduce delays, protect privacy, and simplify administration for the people you care about.

Trusts are not just for wealthy families. They are for people who value clarity, efficiency, and structure.

In rowing terms, a trust is a fully installed system. Rigging is set. Roles are defined. Adjustments are planned. You are not improvising under stress.

Having neither is like showing up to a race without a lineup.

Beneficiaries and Account Titling: Where Most Plans Break Down

One of the most misunderstood parts of estate planning is this.

Many assets do not pass through your will.

Retirement accounts.

Life insurance policies.

Some bank and brokerage accounts.

These assets pass by beneficiary designation.

If beneficiary forms are outdated, incorrect, or missing, your intentions may not matter. Ex-spouses inherit assets. Minor children receive money without structure. Family members are forced into court processes that could have been avoided.

Account titling matters too. How assets are owned determines who can access them, how quickly, and with what tax consequences.

In rowing terms, this is seat assignment.

You can have a great race plan, but if people are in the wrong seats, timing collapses. Confusion shows up exactly when pressure is highest.

Beneficiary mistakes are common, preventable, and costly. Reviewing them regularly is one of the highest-impact actions you can take.

Powers of Attorney: Who Rows When You Cannot

A power of attorney allows someone to act on your behalf if you are unable to.

There are two main types.

Financial power of attorney.

Healthcare power of attorney.

Financial power of attorney allows someone to manage money, pay bills, and handle transactions if you are incapacitated. Healthcare power of attorney allows someone to make medical decisions based on your wishes.

Without these documents, even close family members may be unable to help you. Banks freeze accounts. Medical providers delay decisions. Stress multiplies during moments that are already overwhelming.

In rowing terms, this is your backup seat.

If the stroke goes down, the race does not stop. Someone steps in and keeps the shell moving. Without that plan, everything stalls.

Powers of attorney protect you while you are alive. That is why they matter long before anyone talks about inheritance.

Healthcare Directives: Removing Guesswork Under Pressure

Healthcare directives outline your medical preferences.

End-of-life care.

Life support decisions.

Pain management preferences.

These conversations are uncomfortable. Avoiding them does not protect anyone. It simply shifts the burden to loved ones who are forced to guess under stress.

In rowing terms, this is race strategy for rough conditions.

You do not want your crew debating tactics mid-race. You want clarity before the storm hits.

Healthcare directives reduce conflict, guilt, and uncertainty. They allow loved ones to focus on care, not arguments.

This is not pessimism.

It is preparation.

Why Athletes Delay Estate Planning

Former athletes delay estate planning for predictable reasons.

They feel too young.

They feel healthy.

They assume someone else will handle it.

They do not want to think about worst-case scenarios.

The danger is not that something bad happens immediately.

The danger is that if something happens unexpectedly, everything becomes harder for the people you care about.

Rowers train for conditions they hope never occur.

Estate planning works the same way.

Life Changes Require Updates

Estate planning is not one-and-done.

Marriage.

Divorce.

Children.

Career changes.

Relocation.

Significant asset growth.

Each of these should trigger a review.

In rowing terms, this is adjusting rigging when conditions change. Ignoring updates leads to inefficiency at best and capsizing at worst.

A plan that once made sense can become outdated quietly. Reviewing documents periodically keeps the system aligned with reality.

The Emotional Cost of No Plan

The greatest cost of poor estate planning is not financial.

It is emotional.

Confusion.

Conflict.

Delay.

Stress.

Guilt.

These burdens fall on family members, not on you.

Estate planning is one of the most generous acts you can make. It removes uncertainty and protects relationships when emotions are already high.

That is leadership.

Coach's Perspective

What would your coach say?

Handle your business.

Do not leave it to chance.

Protect the team.

Prepare for what you cannot control.

Clarity beats chaos.

Coaches understand that preparation off the water determines performance when it matters.

Game Situations and Decision Points

You feel healthy.

Do you wait, or do you prepare?

Your life changes.

Do you update documents, or assume they still work?

You want simplicity.

Do you create clarity now, or leave confusion later?

Pressure reveals preparation.

Common Athlete Mistakes and Financial Parallels

Athletes avoid uncomfortable planning.

Financially, that leads to chaos.

Athletes assume someone else will step up.

Financially, that leads to delays and conflict.

Athletes wait too long to adjust.

Financially, that increases cost and stress.

Winning the Long Race

Estate planning is not about predicting the future.

It is about removing uncertainty.

Clear instructions.

Right people.

Right timing.

That is how professionals protect what they build.

You do not wait until race day to assign roles.

You do not wait until crisis to plan your affairs.

Athlete Takeaways

- Estate planning is about control, not age
- Wills and trusts provide structure before pressure hits
- Beneficiary designations matter more than most plans
- Powers of attorney keep the boat moving when you cannot
- Preparation protects the people you care about most

Chapter 24: Talking About Money With Family

Every rower learns this lesson early.

The boat only moves well when everyone understands the plan. If one seat pulls harder, another rushes the slide, or someone ignores the call, speed disappears. Problems do not show up because people are lazy. They show up because expectations were unclear.

Money conversations inside families work the same way.

Most conflict around money is not about dollars. It is about assumptions. Silence. Misaligned expectations. Avoiding conversations until pressure forces them. Former athletes often struggle here because sports environments normalize direct feedback, while families often avoid it.

This chapter is about learning how to communicate around money without blowing up relationships, losing trust, or carrying unnecessary stress.

Teaching Kids About Money: Building Rhythm Early

You do not wait until race day to teach timing.

Kids learn money the same way they learn rowing. Through repetition, observation, and habits modeled consistently. Not through lectures.

Teaching kids about money starts small.

Spending decisions.

Saving for short-term goals.

Understanding tradeoffs.

Delayed gratification.

In rowing terms, this is early technical work. Catch placement. Balance drills. Stroke rhythm. These fundamentals feel simple, but they shape everything later.

Allowances, part-time jobs, and saving goals matter less than the conversations around them. Kids watch how you handle money. They absorb your stress, your confidence, and your habits long before they understand numbers.

Avoid extremes.

Do not shield kids completely.

Do not overwhelm them with adult complexity.

Build comfort with money conversations early so they do not feel taboo later.

College and Young Adults: Loosening the Rigging Without Losing Control

The transition to adulthood mirrors a boat moving from novice to varsity.

More independence.

More responsibility.

More room to make mistakes.

College and early adulthood are often the first time athletes handle money without guardrails. Scholarships, stipends, NIL income, credit cards, and student loans arrive quickly. Financial consequences lag behind behavior.

In rowing terms, this is taking the coxswain mic away while still being in the launch nearby.

Parents struggle here because the instinct to protect clashes with the need to let kids learn. The goal is not control. It is guidance.

Helpful conversations include:

Budgeting expectations.

Credit card use.

Student loans and repayment realities.

Rent and living costs.

Long-term impact of short-term choices.

Avoid rescuing every mistake. Avoid ignoring warning signs. Support growth without removing accountability.

Learning to manage money is part of growing up, not a test to pass perfectly.

Aging Parents and Caregiving: When Roles Reverse Quietly

At some point, roles shift.

Parents who once handled everything may begin needing help. Health changes. Cognitive decline. Financial complexity increases. These transitions are emotional and uncomfortable.

In rowing terms, this is adjusting seats mid-race.

Ignoring the shift does not stop it. It only makes it harder when action becomes unavoidable.

Conversations with aging parents should focus on:

Understanding accounts and bills.

Clarifying estate documents.

Identifying powers of attorney.

Discussing healthcare wishes.

Planning for long-term care scenarios.

These conversations are difficult because they touch identity and independence. Approach them with respect, not control. The goal is preparation, not takeover.

Waiting until a crisis forces decisions removes choice for everyone involved.

Family Expectations and Boundaries: Defining Your Stroke

Money often blurs boundaries.

Who helps whom.

How much support is expected.

What obligations exist.

What is fair.

Families rarely say these things out loud. Assumptions replace communication. Resentment builds quietly.

In rowing terms, this is unclear pressure distribution.

If one seat consistently carries more load without acknowledgment, the boat suffers. Eventually, something breaks.

Setting boundaries is not selfish. It is clarity.

Boundaries might include:

Limits on financial support.

Clear expectations around loans versus gifts.

Conditions tied to assistance.

Protecting your own financial stability.

You cannot support others effectively if you are capsizing yourself. Saying no does not mean you do not care. It means you understand your limits.

Why These Conversations Are Hard for Athletes

Former athletes often avoid family money conversations for familiar reasons.

They do not want conflict.

They assume effort will speak for itself.

They expect fairness without communication.

They believe things will work themselves out.

In sports, structure forces clarity. In families, clarity must be created intentionally.

Avoiding money conversations does not preserve peace. It delays tension until stakes are higher.

Timing Matters More Than Perfection

There is no perfect way to start these conversations.

There is only earlier and later.

Earlier conversations are calmer, more flexible, and easier to adjust. Later conversations are reactive and emotionally charged.

In rowing terms, this is calling adjustments before the boat loses balance instead of after it veers off course.

You do not need all the answers. You need willingness to talk.

Keeping Emotion From Running the Conversation

Money touches identity.

Money touches fear.

Money touches control.

That makes emotions unavoidable.

The goal is not to eliminate emotion. It is to keep it from running the conversation.

Helpful practices include:

Choosing neutral times, not crises.

Using facts, not accusations.

Listening more than talking.

Separating intention from impact.

Revisiting conversations as life changes.

These are the same skills athletes use in team meetings and film review. Honest. Direct. Respectful.

Coach's Perspective

What would your coach say?

Communicate.

Do not assume.

Address issues early.

Protect the team.

Clarity wins.

Coaches know that unspoken tension costs performance long before it becomes visible.

Game Situations and Decision Points

Your child earns income.

Do you avoid the conversation or guide it?

Your parents age.

Do you prepare or wait for crisis?

Family expectations rise.

Do you set boundaries or absorb pressure?

These moments shape relationships and finances.

Common Athlete Mistakes and Financial Parallels

Athletes avoid tough conversations.

Financially, that leads to confusion and resentment.

Athletes assume shared understanding.

Financially, that leads to mismatched expectations.

Athletes overextend for the team.

Financially, that leads to instability.

Winning the Long Race

Money conversations inside families are not one-time events.

They evolve as life changes. New roles emerge. Responsibilities shift. Clear communication keeps relationships intact while protecting financial stability.

Strong crews talk constantly.

Strong families do too.

Athlete Takeaways

- Money problems are usually communication problems
- Teach rhythm early with kids, not lectures later
- Independence requires guidance, not silence
- Boundaries protect the boat, not just the rower
- Clear conversations keep families rowing in sync

Part VI: Crossing the Line Strong

Every rower knows the finish does not take care of itself.

The final stretch of a race is not about discovering new strength. It is about executing what you already trained. Technique either holds or breaks down. Crews that prepared well stay composed. Crews that relied on adrenaline lose form when fatigue hits.

Crossing the line strong in life works the same way.

This final part of the book is not about shortcuts or last-minute heroics. It is about protecting what you have built, avoiding mistakes that erase progress, and making disciplined decisions when stakes are highest.

Why Finishing Well Is Different Than Starting Fast

Most athletes know how to start strong.

They understand sacrifice.

They know how to push.

They are comfortable with discomfort.

What fewer athletes are taught is how to *finish* well.

In rowing, races are often lost in the final third because fatigue exposes weak preparation. Timing slips. Communication fades. Panic replaces rhythm.

Financial lives follow the same pattern.

People work hard early, save, and invest. Later, complexity increases. Taxes matter more. Family responsibilities grow. Legal and planning decisions carry more weight. This is where mistakes are most expensive.

Crossing the line strong means recognizing that the race changes near the end and adjusting accordingly.

When Doing Everything Yourself Stops Working

Early in the race, rowing is individual.

You focus on your seat.

You build fitness.

You learn technique.

Later, attention shifts to the boat as a whole. Coordination matters more than raw power.

Money works the same way.

Early on, managing things yourself often makes sense. Accounts are simple. Decisions are limited. Errors are recoverable. Over time, complexity grows. The cost of mistakes increases. Strength alone is no longer enough.

This is when structure, planning, and the right support become critical.

Knowing when to stop rowing alone is not weakness. It is awareness.

Avoiding the Late-Race Mistakes

Most financial damage does not come from laziness.

It comes from:

Urgency

Overconfidence

Fear

Silence

Scams succeed because they create pressure.

Bad advice spreads because it sounds confident.

Costly mistakes persist because people avoid asking questions.

In rowing terms, this is rushing the finish.

Crews that sprint blindly lose balance. Crews that stay composed gain ground quietly.

Finishing well requires slowing down when pressure rises, not speeding up emotionally.

Defense Wins Late

Early in races, offense gets attention.

Late in races, defense wins.

Protecting the lead.

Avoiding unforced errors.

Managing risk.

Preserving form.

Financially, this stage emphasizes protection.

Avoiding scams.

Managing taxes.

Updating documents.

Protecting relationships.

Maintaining discipline.

None of this is exciting. All of it is decisive.

Sloppy finishes erase strong starts.

Crossing the Line Is Not the End

Crossing the line does not mean the journey stops.

After the finish comes recovery, reflection, and adjustment. Financial stability and independence are not static achievements. They require maintenance and awareness as life continues to change.

The goal is not perfection.

The goal is control.

What It Means to Finish Strong

Finishing strong means:

You understand your plan.

You trust your structure.

You know who is in your boat.
You are not reacting emotionally.
You protect what you built.
In rowing terms, it means clean blades through the line.
This book is not about winning one race.
It is about rowing well for a lifetime.
Finish with discipline.
Finish with clarity.
Finish strong.

Chapter 25: Advisors, Scams, and Long-Term Success

Every rower eventually reaches a point where effort alone is not enough.

Early on, you can rely on raw fitness. You pull hard, follow simple instruction, and improve quickly. As competition increases, details matter more. Technique, rigging, recovery, strategy, and decision-making all start to separate crews that merely work hard from crews that win consistently.

No serious rowing program operates without a support team.

There are coaches, launch drivers, riggers, strength staff, and medical professionals. Not because the athletes are weak, but because the race gets more complex. The same principle applies to money.

Long-term financial success is not about doing everything yourself forever. It is about knowing when to bring in help, who to trust, and how to avoid the people and decisions that can flip the boat late in the race.

When to Seek Professional Help

You do not wait until you miss a race to talk to a coach.

Professional financial help makes sense when complexity increases. That does not mean you failed. It means the race changed.

Common signals include:

Rising income

Multiple investment accounts

Tax complexity

Insurance decisions

Family responsibilities

Business ownership

Estate planning needs

In rowing terms, this is moving from single sculls to a crew boat. Coordination matters more. Mistakes affect more people.

Trying to muscle through complexity alone often leads to errors that compound quietly. Seeking help is not giving up control. It is protecting momentum.

The right time to ask for help is before pressure forces you to.

Types of Financial Advisors: Know Who Is in the Launch

Not all advisors play the same role.

Some focus primarily on investments.

Some focus on holistic planning.

Some sell financial products.

Some coordinate across taxes, insurance, investments, and estate planning.

Understanding how advisors are compensated matters. Fees, commissions, and incentives influence behavior. Alignment matters more than titles.

In rowing terms, this is knowing who is actually steering.

A good advisor should:

Explain clearly

Listen more than talk

Show how decisions connect

Encourage discipline

Reduce stress, not increase it

A bad advisor:

Creates urgency

Promises certainty

Avoids transparency

Pushes products before understanding context

You do not hand the coxswain mic to someone you do not trust. The same applies financially.

Recognizing Scams and Bad Advice

Scams target emotion, not intelligence.

They rely on:

Urgency

Exclusivity

Guaranteed outcomes

Pressure to act quickly

Promises that bypass discipline

If something sounds too good to be true, it almost always is.

In rowing terms, this is biting on every pump fake. Discipline keeps you upright. Impulse flips the boat.

Bad advice is often louder than good advice. It is confident. Simple. Emotional. It promises shortcuts.

Real financial progress is quiet.

Boring.

Repeatable.

If secrecy is required, speed is demanded, or questions are discouraged, step away.

Ten Common Financial Mistakes

Most financial damage comes from predictable patterns, not rare events.

1. Chasing quick wins instead of building consistency
2. Ignoring taxes until they become painful
3. Overspending early when income increases
4. Delaying saving and investing because it feels distant
5. Concentrating too much risk in one area

6. Avoiding uncomfortable planning conversations
7. Trusting the wrong people without verification
8. Letting emotion dictate decisions
9. Failing to set boundaries with money
10. Doing nothing out of fear of making a mistake

In rowing terms, these are technical flaws repeated over thousands of strokes. One mistake rarely sinks you. Repetition does.

Awareness prevents most of them.

Ten Rules for Long-Term Success

Long-term success is built on principles, not predictions.

1. Live below your means
2. Save consistently, not occasionally
3. Invest with discipline, not excitement
4. Diversify risk intentionally
5. Manage taxes proactively
6. Protect yourself with appropriate insurance
7. Keep systems simple and repeatable
8. Communicate clearly with family and partners
9. Adjust as life changes
10. Stay patient and committed

These rules are not exciting.

They work.

In rowing terms, this is clean technique held under fatigue. Not flashy. Highly effective.

Why Athletes Are Vulnerable Late in the Race

Former athletes are competitive, confident, and action-oriented. Those traits help early. They can hurt later.

Confidence turns into overconfidence.

Competitiveness turns into comparison.

Action turns into overtrading.

Late-race mistakes often come from abandoning discipline because progress already feels earned.

In rowing terms, this is celebrating before the line.

The race is not over until it is over.

The Role of Advisors in the Long Race

A good advisor does not row for you.

They help you:

Stay balanced

Avoid unforced errors

Stick to your plan

Adjust when life changes

Protect what you built

They act like a coach in the launch. Calm. Observant. Focused on long-term outcomes, not short-term noise.

The wrong advisor creates dependency.

The right one creates confidence.

Coach's Perspective

What would your coach say?

Know who you trust.

Do not chase shortcuts.

Stay disciplined.

Protect the boat.

Finish what you started.

Coaches know that championships are lost by panic and ego more than lack of effort.

Game Situations and Decision Points

You are offered a "can't-miss" opportunity.

Do you slow down or rush?

Your finances get more complex.

Do you seek help or guess?

Pressure rises late.

Do you trust your structure or react emotionally?

These moments define outcomes.

Winning the Long Race

Long-term success is not built on brilliance.

It is built on:

Consistency

Discipline

Good support

Avoiding obvious mistakes

You do not need to be perfect.

You need to stay in the boat.

Rowers who finish strong do not rely on adrenaline. They rely on preparation, trust, and composure.

That is how long races are won.

Athlete Takeaways

- You do not row championships alone, and you should not manage complexity alone
- Know who is steering before you trust the launch

- Urgency and guarantees are warning signs
- Small mistakes repeated quietly cause the most damage
- Discipline and patience win long races

Chapter 26: Losing the Schedule and Rebuilding Structure

Every rower remembers the first time the schedule disappeared.

During the season, everything is planned. Morning rows. Lifts. Erg pieces. Film review. Travel. Team meetings. The calendar tells you where to be and when to show up. Discipline is built into the system. You do not debate whether to train. You just do it.

Then the boat is docked.

No practice times. No coach watching the clock. No teammate knocking on your door for early rows. What used to be mandatory becomes optional, and that shift quietly changes everything.

Life after sports gets harder not because you lost discipline, but because the structure that enforced it is gone.

From Mandatory Workouts to Optional Discipline

In rowing, discipline is external.

Miss a practice and it is noticed. Skip a lift and it shows up in the boat. Fall behind and your seat is at risk. The environment forces consistency even on days when motivation is low.

After sports, discipline becomes internal.

You can skip workouts.

You can delay saving.

You can ignore planning.

You can push things to "later."

Nothing bad happens immediately.

That delay is dangerous.

In rowing terms, this is open water without a coach launch nearby. You can row hard, or you can drift. The water does not punish you right away, but over time, direction disappears.

Optional discipline is harder than mandatory discipline. It requires intention, not just effort.

Why the Absence of Structure Breaks Financial Habits

Most former athletes do not suddenly become irresponsible.

They drift.

Saving becomes inconsistent.

Bills get paid late.

Budgets become loose suggestions.

Long-term goals fade into background noise.

There is no dramatic failure. Just slow erosion.

In rowing terms, this is losing rhythm stroke by stroke. Each stroke feels fine on its own. Over distance, the boat loses speed and direction.

Money habits depend heavily on structure. When structure disappears, habits rely on motivation. Motivation is unreliable.

Athletes are conditioned to respond to accountability. When accountability disappears, behavior changes unless systems replace it.

Why Former Athletes Struggle More Than They Expect

Athletes are used to high standards.

They push through discomfort.

They show up tired.

They perform under pressure.

That makes the transition deceptive. You assume discipline will carry over automatically. But discipline in sports was supported by environment.

Remove the environment, and the discipline has to be rebuilt differently.

In rowing terms, this is rowing without a coxswain.

You are still strong.

You still know technique.

But someone must call the rate, manage rhythm, and keep direction.

After sports, that someone is you.

Replacing Practice Schedules With Personal Systems

Structure does not disappear.

It must be rebuilt.

Personal systems replace practice schedules.

Automatic transfers for saving and investing.

Scheduled check-ins with finances.

Calendar blocks for workouts and recovery.

Rules that remove decision-making.

In rowing terms, this is creating your own training plan.

You decide when to row.

When to lift.

When to rest.

When to review performance.

The goal is not rigidity.

The goal is rhythm.

Systems reduce the need for motivation. They make good behavior the default.

If saving requires constant decision-making, it will eventually stop. If it happens automatically, it continues even when life gets busy.

The Difference Between Freedom and Drift

Many former athletes confuse freedom with lack of structure.

Freedom feels good at first.

No alarms.

No mandatory sessions.

No one tracking attendance.

Over time, freedom without structure becomes drift.

In rowing terms, this is rowing without a course.

You are moving.

You are working.

But you are not necessarily going anywhere.

True freedom comes from structure you choose, not structure you escape.

When systems are in place, flexibility increases. You can adjust without falling apart. Without systems, every disruption causes chaos.

Financial Structure Is About Reducing Friction

Good systems reduce friction.

Bills get paid automatically.

Savings happens before spending.

Investments continue regardless of mood.

Reviews happen on a schedule, not during panic.

In rowing terms, this is clean rigging.

When equipment is set properly, effort transfers efficiently. When it is not, every stroke costs more energy.

Financial structure does the same thing. It allows the same income to go farther with less stress.

Why Grind Culture Fails Without Structure

Many former athletes try to replace structure with intensity.

They work longer hours.

They push harder.

They sacrifice recovery.

This works briefly.

Then burnout arrives.

In rowing terms, this is rowing every session at race pace.

You feel productive.

You feel tough.

You break down.

Adult life rewards sustainability, not constant grind. The goal is not to recreate athletic intensity. It is to create repeatable discipline.

Structure supports sustainability.

Grind culture destroys it.

How Structure Protects You During Life Transitions

Life disruptions expose weak systems.

Job changes.

Moves.

Family responsibilities.

Health issues.

When structure is external, transitions break habits. When structure is internal and system-based, habits survive.

In rowing terms, this is training through different conditions.

Crews with good fundamentals adjust.

Crews without them fall apart.

Building structure early protects you later.

Coach's Perspective

What would your coach say?

Nobody is setting your schedule now.

That does not mean it does not matter.

Discipline is your responsibility.

Build structure or drift.

Show up anyway.

Coaches know that effort without structure fades quickly.

Game Situations and Decision Points

You have flexibility.

Do you use it intentionally or waste it?

You miss a habit.

Do you reset or quit?

No one is watching.

Do you show up anyway?

These moments determine outcomes.

Common Athlete Mistakes and Financial Parallels

Athletes rely on external accountability.

Financially, that leads to inconsistency.

Athletes underestimate drift.

Financially, that leads to lost progress.

Athletes avoid systems.

Financially, that leads to chaos.

Winning the Long Race

Rebuilding structure after sports is one of the most important skills former athletes must learn.

Systems replace coaches.

Calendars replace practice plans.

Discipline becomes internal.

Those who rebuild structure early protect their future.

Those who do not often wonder why life feels harder than it should.

The boat does not move itself.

Neither does your financial life.

Athlete Takeaways

- Losing the schedule creates hidden risk
- Optional discipline is harder than mandatory discipline
- Drift breaks habits quietly
- Systems replace motivation
- Build structure or lose direction

Chapter 27: From Teammates to Coworkers

Every rower knows the feeling of stepping into a boathouse for the first time.

You do not yet know the personalities. You do not know who sets the tone. You do not know how decisions get made. Over time, that uncertainty disappears. Roles become clear. The coxswain calls the race. The stroke sets rhythm. Coaches give direction. Feedback is constant. Effort is visible.

Then sports end, and you enter the workplace.

Suddenly, the structure you trained inside for years is gone. The rules feel different. Authority is unclear. Feedback is inconsistent. Performance is harder to measure. For many former athletes, this transition is more disorienting than the physical end of competition.

This shift affects more than job satisfaction. It directly impacts income growth, confidence, and long-term career stability.

Why the Workplace Feels Foreign After Sports

Sports environments are built on clarity.

If you perform, you race.

If you do not, you sit.

If you improve, your seat changes.

The feedback loop is tight and honest.

Workplaces rarely function that way.

Performance metrics are vague. Expectations shift. Promotions do not always go to the best performer. Effort is often invisible. Politics and perception play larger roles than most athletes expect.

In rowing terms, this is racing without a finish line clock.

You are pulling hard, but you are not sure how you are being judged or where you stand.

Former athletes often struggle because they assume performance alone will be enough. In many workplaces, it is not.

Authority Without Coaches

In rowing, authority is obvious.

Coaches decide lineups.

Coxswains call strategy.

Captains set standards.

Accountability is enforced.

In the workplace, authority is less visible.

Managers may avoid confrontation.

Decision-making may happen behind closed doors.

Influence does not always align with titles.

Understanding who actually makes decisions matters more than org charts.

Former athletes often wait for direction because that is how sports worked. In the workplace, waiting can stall progress. Initiative is expected but rarely explained.

In rowing terms, this is being in a shell with no clear coxswain. Someone is steering. You just need to figure out who.

Feedback Without Film

Athletes are conditioned by film.

You see mistakes immediately.

You correct them quickly.

Feedback is specific and frequent.

In the workplace, feedback is often delayed, indirect, or avoided entirely.

You may not hear anything until review time.

You may be underperforming without knowing it.

You may be doing well without recognition.

In rowing terms, this is training without video review.

You have to feel your mistakes instead of seeing them. That requires self-awareness and proactive communication.

Former athletes who succeed learn to ask for feedback instead of waiting for it. They schedule check-ins. They clarify expectations. They do not assume silence means approval.

Politics, Ambiguity, and Unclear Expectations

Workplaces include politics whether you like it or not.

Relationships matter.

Timing matters.

Perception matters.

This feels uncomfortable for athletes raised in merit-based systems. In sports, effort and results are visible. In work, contribution is often filtered through communication and relationships.

Ignoring politics does not make them disappear.

Navigating them professionally does not mean compromising values. It means understanding the environment you are operating in.

In rowing terms, this is adjusting to conditions.

You do not fight the current.

You do not ignore the wind.

You adjust your stroke and steering.

Former athletes who refuse to adapt often feel frustrated and stuck. Those who learn the environment protect opportunity and income.

How This Impacts Income Growth and Career Stability

Confusion slows progress.

When expectations are unclear, you may focus on the wrong priorities. When feedback is missing, improvement stalls. When politics are ignored, opportunities pass quietly.

This leads to slower income growth, missed promotions, and instability.

Former athletes who adapt tend to advance faster.

They seek clarity.

They build relationships.

They communicate goals.

They advocate for themselves.

They treat their career like a long race, not a single piece.

Those who do not adapt often job hop, disengage, or blame systems they never learned to navigate.

Translating Athletic Skills to the Workplace

The skills you developed in sports still matter.

Preparation.

Discipline.

Coachability.

Team awareness.

Mental toughness.

They just apply differently.

In rowing terms, the stroke changes, but the fundamentals remain.

You still need rhythm.

You still need awareness.

You still need to respond to conditions.

The mistake is expecting the workplace to look like the boathouse. The opportunity is using what the boathouse taught you to succeed somewhere new.

Coach's Perspective

What would your coach say?

Learn the system.

Communicate clearly.

Ask for feedback.

Do your job.

Take ownership.

Nobody is managing your development now except you.

Game Situations and Decision Points

You are unsure what matters most in your role.

Do you ask for clarity or guess?

You want advancement.

Do you wait to be noticed or advocate for yourself?

You feel frustrated by politics.

Do you disengage or learn the environment?

These choices shape income and stability.

Common Athlete Mistakes and Financial Parallels

Athletes wait for direction.

Financially, that stalls income growth.

Athletes avoid politics.

Financially, that limits opportunity.

Athletes expect fairness.

Financially, that leads to frustration.

Winning the Long Race

The workplace is not the locker room.

The rules are different.

The feedback loop is slower.

The authority structure is less visible.

But success is still possible.

Former athletes who adapt without losing discipline build stable, growing careers. They stop waiting for the whistle. They learn the system. They stay proactive.

The race did not end.

The course changed.

Athlete Takeaways

- The workplace lacks the clarity of sports
- Authority and feedback are less visible
- Politics and perception affect opportunity
- Communication protects income growth
- Adaptation builds long-term career stability

Chapter 28: When No One Is Watching Anymore

Every rower knows the difference between race day and practice.

On race day, the boathouse is loud. Coaches are watching. Teammates are locked in. There is a clock, a finish line, and consequences. You show up prepared because accountability is unavoidable.

Then there are the quiet days.

Early mornings. Empty docks. No spectators. No pressure except the one you bring yourself.

After sports, life becomes one long version of those quiet days.

No crowd.

No coach.

No lineup.

No scoreboard.

What disappears is not discipline. It is enforced accountability. And that gap quietly changes everything.

The Discipline Gap After Accountability Disappears

In sports, discipline is built into the environment.

Miss a workout and someone notices.

Skip practice and your seat changes.

Slack on preparation and it shows immediately.

Structure forces consistency.

After sports, that structure vanishes.

You can skip saving.

Delay investing.

Ignore budgeting.

Postpone planning.

Nothing happens right away.

That delay is dangerous.

In rowing terms, this is training alone without a coach timing pieces. You can tell yourself you are working hard, but effort drifts without feedback or consequence.

Most former athletes do not lose discipline overnight. They lose urgency. The consequences of financial decisions are delayed, so mistakes feel harmless in the moment.

Why Former Athletes Self-Sabotage Without Pressure

Pressure sharpens focus.

It forces preparation.

It narrows attention.

It demands execution.

Without pressure, comfort creeps in.

Netflix replaces workouts.

Eating out replaces budgeting.

Impulse spending replaces saving.

Short-term relief replaces long-term progress.

Self-sabotage is rarely intentional. It shows up as drift.

Former athletes are used to external pressure doing the heavy lifting. When that pressure disappears, many struggle to manufacture urgency on their own.

In rowing terms, this is settling into an easy stroke rate because no one is calling splits. The boat still moves, but it is not going anywhere fast.

Comfort feels earned.

Growth still requires effort.

Comfort vs Growth Decisions

Every financial decision sits on a spectrum between comfort and growth.

Comfort feels good now.

Growth feels uncomfortable now but pays off later.

Comfort looks like:

- Spending to relieve stress
- Delaying saving because "later is fine"
- Avoiding uncomfortable conversations about money
- Ignoring planning because it feels overwhelming

Growth looks like:

- Saving before spending
- Saying no when no one is forcing you
- Building systems instead of relying on motivation
- Making boring decisions consistently

In rowing terms, comfort is dropping the rate early because it feels sustainable. Growth is holding pace when it burns, knowing it pays off later.

Money mistakes often come from choosing comfort repeatedly. The cost does not show up immediately. It shows up years later when options are limited.

Translating "Grind Culture" Into Adult Life

Grind culture does not translate cleanly outside of sports.

In athletics, intensity is rewarded.

In adult life, consistency is rewarded.

Former athletes often try to recreate competitive intensity without structure. They work harder instead of smarter. They chase hustle instead of systems. Burnout follows.

Adult success is not about constant grind.

It is about sustainable discipline.

Automatic contributions.

Scheduled reviews.

Clear rules.

Simple plans.

In rowing terms, this is learning to row efficiently instead of muscling every stroke. Long races are not won by pulling harder. They are won by rhythm, timing, and endurance.

The goal is not to live at race intensity forever.

The goal is to build habits that last.

Why Money Mistakes Show Up Years Later

Money has delayed feedback.

Overspending today creates stress years later.

Skipping saving now limits options later.

Ignoring investing early costs decades of compounding.

In sports, mistakes are immediate.

In money, mistakes compound quietly.

In rowing terms, this is washing out early in a piece. You may not feel it immediately, but it shows up in the final 500 meters when the boat fades.

Former athletes are conditioned for immediate feedback. When it disappears, decision-making often suffers.

Just because nothing happened today does not mean nothing happened.

Rebuilding Accountability Without a Coach

Accountability does not disappear. It has to be rebuilt.

Systems replace coaches.

Calendars replace practice plans.

Rules replace whistles.

Examples:

- Automatic transfers instead of manual saving
- Scheduled check-ins instead of reactive reviews
- Clear spending rules instead of "feeling it out"
- Long-term goals written down instead of assumed

In rowing terms, this is self-coached training. You set the workouts. You time the pieces. You hold yourself to standards even when no one is watching.

The goal is not perfection.

The goal is rhythm.

The Illusion of Freedom

Many former athletes mistake the absence of structure for freedom.

No practice.

No meetings.

No rules.

But unstructured freedom often becomes drift.

In rowing terms, removing the coxswain does not automatically make the boat faster. Without direction, it wanders.

Discipline creates freedom.

Structure creates options.

Consistency creates confidence.

When you rebuild structure, decisions become easier. Anxiety decreases. Progress becomes visible again.

Coach's Perspective

What would your coach say?

Nobody is watching now.

That does not mean it does not matter.

Discipline is your responsibility.

Do not drift.

Choose growth.

Championship habits are built in empty boathouses.

Game Situations and Decision Points

You are tired after work.

Do you choose comfort or discipline?

No one notices your financial habits.

Do you show up anyway?

The payoff feels far away.

Do you stay consistent or quit early?

What you do when no one is watching defines outcomes.

Common Athlete Mistakes and Financial Parallels

Athletes rely on external pressure.

Financially, that leads to drift.

Athletes chase comfort.

Financially, that leads to overspending.

Athletes confuse grind with progress.

Financially, that leads to burnout.

Winning the Long Race

Discipline without an audience is harder, but it is more powerful.

The habits you maintain privately shape the results you see publicly. Former athletes who rebuild structure early protect their future. Those who do not often wonder where momentum went.

The race did not end.

The crowd just left.

What matters now is how you row when it is quiet.

Athlete Takeaways

- Accountability disappears after sports
- Discipline must become internal
- Comfort choices compound into problems
- Systems beat grind culture
- What you do when no one is watching matters most

Chapter 29: Redefining Winning After the Uniform Comes Off

For most of your athletic life, winning was obvious.

Finish times.

Seat races.

Lineups.

Medals.

Championships.

Rowing is brutally honest. The boat moves or it does not. The clock does not lie. You know exactly where you stand because performance is measured every day.

Then the uniform comes off.

The metrics disappear, but the competitive instinct does not. Many former athletes feel restless not because they stopped caring, but because they no longer know how to measure progress. When performance is no longer clearly defined, something else quietly takes its place.

Status.

Why Chasing Status Replaces Chasing Performance

In sports, performance is the currency.

You earn your seat.

You earn your minutes.

You earn trust through output.

After sports, performance becomes harder to see. Effort is less visible. Feedback is delayed or vague. Progress is no longer measured in seconds or splits.

So many former athletes default to what can be seen.

Income.

Job titles.

Homes.

Cars.

Lifestyle.

These things look like winning, especially from the outside.

In rowing terms, this is racing other boats without a clock. When you cannot measure your own pace, you start watching everyone else. Instead of rowing your race, you row reactively.

Status provides short-term validation.

Performance provides long-term fulfillment.

When former athletes lose the performance scoreboard, they often chase symbols that resemble it.

Income vs Fulfillment

Income matters. It creates stability, options, and security. Pretending otherwise is naive.

But income alone is not fulfillment.

Many former athletes reach income goals and still feel unsettled. The structure is gone. The clarity is gone. The daily sense of progress feels muted.

In rowing terms, this is winning a heat but feeling disconnected from the race. The result looks good, but something feels off.

Fulfillment comes from alignment, not just achievement.

Growth.

Contribution.

Control over time.

Health.

Purpose.

Progress toward meaningful goals.

Income supports those things.

It does not replace them.

When income becomes the only scoreboard, decisions start drifting. People take jobs they hate to maintain appearances. They overspend to keep up. They sacrifice flexibility for status.

That is not winning.

That is surviving with pressure.

Titles, Houses, Cars, and Comparison Traps

Comparison is relentless.

Social media amplifies it.

Former teammates become measuring sticks.

Career paths diverge and get ranked in your head.

Titles feel like proof.

Homes feel like milestones.

Cars feel like rewards.

But these symbols rarely deliver what they promise.

In rowing terms, this is chasing another boat's rhythm instead of trusting your own stroke. You burn energy reacting instead of rowing efficiently.

Lifestyle inflation is one of the most common traps for former athletes. As income increases, spending expands to match perceived success. The pressure never ends because there is always someone ahead.

Comparison creates urgency.

Urgency creates bad decisions.

When choices are driven by how things look instead of how they function, fulfillment erodes quietly.

What "Success" Actually Looks Like in Your 30s and 40s

Success evolves.

In your early twenties, success often looks like opportunity.

In your thirties and forties, it starts to look like stability and control.

Real success often includes:

- Flexibility in how you use your time
- Financial stability without constant stress
- Health and energy
- Strong relationships
- The ability to say no
- Confidence in your direction

These wins do not show up on LinkedIn.

They do not photograph well.

They do not impress strangers.

In rowing terms, this is rowing efficiently over a long piece instead of sprinting early for attention. The finish matters more than the early splash.

Former athletes who redefine success early make better decisions. They choose roles that fit their lives. They build savings quietly. They invest consistently. They stop chasing validation and start building alignment.

Those who do not often feel like they are working hard but going nowhere.

Building a New Scoreboard

You cannot win a race if you do not know how it is scored.

After sports, you need a new scoreboard.

Examples of meaningful metrics:

- Peace of mind
- Net worth growth over time
- Consistency in saving and investing

- Control over your schedule
- Reduced financial anxiety
- Alignment between values and decisions
- Progress toward long-term independence

In rowing terms, this is setting your own splits for a long training piece. You decide the pace. You track what matters. You stop reacting to other boats.

Without a personal scoreboard, it is easy to confuse motion with progress.

Busy does not mean winning.

Expensive does not mean successful.

Visible does not mean fulfilled.

The Cost of Playing the Wrong Game

Many former athletes are still competing.

They are just competing in the wrong game.

They chase:

- Higher income without lifestyle control
- Bigger houses without flexibility
- Recognition without satisfaction

The cost shows up as stress, burnout, and regret.

In rowing terms, this is rowing the wrong course perfectly. You execute well, but you end up somewhere you never wanted to be.

Redefining winning is not lowering standards.

It is raising them.

It requires honesty.

It requires introspection.

It requires stepping away from comparison.

Coach's Perspective

What would your coach say?
Define your race.
Stop looking sideways.
Trust your training.
Row your pace.
Finish strong.
You cannot win someone else's race.
You can only win your own.

Game Situations and Decision Points

You see a former teammate's lifestyle online.
Do you compare or refocus?
You hit an income milestone.
Do you ask what is next or what actually matters?
You feel pressure to upgrade your life.
Do you chase status or protect alignment?
The scoreboard you choose determines the race you run.

Common Athlete Mistakes and Financial Parallels

Athletes chase validation.
Financially, that leads to overspending.
Athletes avoid reflection.
Financially, that leads to misaligned goals.
Athletes confuse visibility with winning.
Financially, that leads to regret.

Winning the Long Race

Redefining winning does not mean abandoning ambition.

It means directing it.

When success aligns with who you are and how you want to live, the pressure eases. Decisions get cleaner. Progress becomes sustainable.

Rowing teaches this better than most sports.

Long races reward patience.

Efficiency beats force.

Rhythm beats chaos.

The uniform may be gone, but the competitor is still there. The challenge now is choosing the right race and scoring it correctly.

Athlete Takeaways

- Status is not the same as winning
- Income supports fulfillment but does not replace it
- Comparison distorts decision-making
- Success evolves with life stages
- Build a new scoreboard that reflects what actually matters

Chapter 30: Staying Connected Without Living in the Past

One of the quietest losses after sports is not competition.

It is connection.

When you rowed, you were never alone. Even in silence, you were surrounded by people moving in the same direction. Early mornings. Shared suffering. Inside jokes. Accountability without explanation. The boat demanded presence, and the team created identity.

Then the season ends.

The boat is docked.

The boathouse gets quieter.

Daily contact fades. Group texts slow down. Everyone scatters into careers, cities, and new routines. Many former athletes underestimate how much of their stability came from simply being part of something structured and shared.

Staying connected matters.

Living in the past does not.

The challenge after sports is learning how to do one without falling into the other.

The Role of Community, Mentorship, and New Locker Rooms

Rowing thrives on community.

You do not row well in isolation. Timing matters. Trust matters. Accountability matters. Even the strongest athlete cannot move a shell efficiently alone. Progress comes from shared rhythm.

After sports, that built-in community disappears unless you intentionally rebuild it.

New locker rooms exist, but they look different:

- Work teams
- Professional organizations
- Volunteer groups
- Faith communities
- Alumni networks
- Peer groups of former athletes
- Mentorship relationships

These environments replace what the boathouse once provided: structure, feedback, and belonging.

Mentorship becomes especially important. Learning from people a few steps ahead shortens the learning curve. It prevents unnecessary mistakes. It provides perspective when things feel disorienting.

In rowing terms, this is joining a new crew after switching programs. The rigging is different. The calls change. But the fundamentals still apply. You just need to learn the new rhythm.

The mistake is waiting for community to appear.

Connection has to be built.

Why Isolation Hits Former Athletes Hard

Isolation rarely shows up as loneliness at first.

It shows up as overwork.

Disengagement.

Loss of motivation.

Short temper.

Restlessness.

Drifting habits.

Former athletes go from constant interaction to mostly solo schedules almost overnight. What once felt normal suddenly feels quiet, even when life is busy.

In rowing terms, this is rowing without communication. No calls. No feedback. No correction. The boat still moves, but inefficiency creeps in quietly.

Isolation narrows perspective. Without teammates or trusted voices, small problems feel bigger. Bad decisions go unchecked. Motivation fades without accountability.

Many former athletes try to handle this by staying busy instead of staying connected. That works for a while. Eventually, the lack of shared purpose shows up.

Connection is not a luxury.

It is infrastructure.

Finding Purpose Without the Team

Purpose does not disappear when the team does.

It changes.

Athletes who struggle most after sports are often still chasing the exact feeling competition gave them instead of building a new version of it. They want the same rush, the same identity, the same validation.

That exact experience does not come back.

Something better can replace it.

Purpose after sports often comes from:

- Leadership
- Teaching
- Mentoring
- Building something meaningful
- Serving others
- Creating stability for family
- Developing mastery in a new field

In rowing terms, this is adjusting your role as the lineup changes. You are no longer the same athlete you were at 19 or 22. That does not mean you are less valuable. It means your contribution looks different.

Purpose comes from impact, not applause.

When former athletes stop chasing the past version of purpose and start building a forward-facing one, clarity returns.

Healthy Nostalgia vs Being Stuck

Nostalgia is normal.

You should remember your rowing days.

You should appreciate them.

They shaped who you are.

The danger is living there.

Healthy nostalgia honors the past without letting it define the future. Being stuck shows up when identity stops evolving.

Warning signs include:

- Every story ends with what you used to do
- Current goals feel vague or unmotivating
- New opportunities are constantly compared to the past
- You avoid fully committing to the present
- You feel like your best days are behind you

In rowing terms, this is replaying old races instead of preparing for the next piece. Reflection becomes a substitute for growth.

The past should inform you.

It should not trap you.

Creating a Forward-Looking Identity

Identity has to move forward.

You are not an athlete who used to row.

You are a person who learned discipline, resilience, teamwork, and endurance through rowing.

Those skills still matter.

They just need a new outlet.

A forward-looking identity focuses on:

- Who you are becoming
- What you are building
- How you want to contribute
- What kind of life you want to live

In rowing terms, this is transferring skills to a new shell. The stroke is familiar. The environment is different. The fundamentals still win.

Former athletes who build forward-looking identity stop asking, "Who was I?" and start asking, "Who am I becoming?"

That shift changes everything.

Coach's Perspective

What would your coach say?

Honor the past.

Show up in the present.

Commit to the next phase.

Stay connected.

Keep rowing.

The real failure is not leaving sports.

It is stopping growth.

Game Situations and Decision Points

You feel disconnected.

Do you isolate or seek community?

You miss the team environment.

Do you rebuild structure or live in memory?

You define yourself by the past.

Do you evolve or stay stuck?

Connection shapes identity, whether you choose it intentionally or not.

Common Athlete Mistakes and Financial Parallels

Athletes cling to past identity.

Financially, that leads to stagnation.

Athletes isolate.

Financially, that leads to poor decisions and missed opportunities.

Athletes avoid change.

Financially, that limits growth and flexibility.

Winning the Long Race

Staying connected does not mean staying the same.

Growth requires new relationships, new roles, and new definitions of purpose. Former athletes who thrive after sports are not the ones who forget the past. They are the ones who integrate it into something bigger.

Rowing teaches this better than most sports.

Long races require rhythm.

Crews change.

Conditions shift.

The finish line moves.
The game continues.
Just in a different form.

Athlete Takeaways

- Community matters long after competition ends
- Isolation quietly erodes motivation and clarity
- Purpose evolves beyond the team
- Honor the past without living in it
- Build a forward-looking identity and keep rowing forward

Glossary of Rowing and Financial Terms

This glossary connects key financial concepts to familiar ideas from **rowing**, making money easier to understand through the language, structure, rhythm, and discipline rowers already know.

Asset Allocation

Financial Definition:

How money is divided among different investment types such as stocks, bonds, and cash to balance risk and return.

Rowing Comparison:

Seat balance in the shell. If too much power or responsibility is loaded into one seat, the boat loses balance and efficiency. Proper distribution keeps the shell running clean over long distances.

Assets

Financial Definition:

Things you own that have value, such as cash, investments, real estate, or retirement accounts.

Rowing Comparison:

Your strengths as a rower. Technique, conditioning, endurance, experience, and discipline that contribute to overall boat speed.

Bonds

Financial Definition:

Loans made to governments or companies that pay interest and return principal over time.

Rowing Comparison:

Steady base pressure. Not flashy, but essential for control and stability when conditions get rough.

Budget

Financial Definition:

A plan for how income is allocated toward expenses, savings, and goals.

Rowing Comparison:

The stroke rate plan. If you do not know your rate, you burn out early or lose rhythm.

Cash Flow

Financial Definition:

Money coming in versus money going out.

Rowing Comparison:

Energy management during a race. Spend too much early and you fade before the finish.

Compounding

Financial Definition:

Earnings that generate additional earnings over time.

Rowing Comparison:

Consistent training volume. Each practice builds on the last, and progress accelerates with time.

Credit

Financial Definition:

The ability to borrow money with the promise of repayment.

Rowing Comparison:

Trust within the crew. When earned and managed well, it creates opportunity. When abused, it disrupts rhythm.

Debt

Financial Definition:

Money borrowed that must be repaid, often with interest.

Rowing Comparison:

Added drag. Manageable in small amounts, dangerous when excessive.

Diversification

Financial Definition:

Spreading investments across different assets to reduce risk.

Rowing Comparison:

Not relying on one rower or one stroke to carry the boat. Depth and balance keep the shell upright.

Emergency Fund

Financial Definition:

Savings set aside for unexpected expenses.

Rowing Comparison:

A spare oar or launch nearby. You hope you never need it, but it prevents disaster when something breaks.

ETF (Exchange-Traded Fund)

Financial Definition:

A fund that holds many investments and trades like a stock.

Rowing Comparison:

A crew shell instead of a single. Shared effort spreads risk and increases efficiency.

Fees / Expense Ratios

Financial Definition:

Costs associated with managing investments.

Rowing Comparison:

Poor rigging or sloppy catches. Small inefficiencies that quietly slow the boat over time.

Growth Investing

Financial Definition:

Investing in companies expected to grow faster than average.

Rowing Comparison:

High-rate racing. More upside, but it demands strong technique and discipline.

Insurance

Financial Definition:

Protection against financial loss from unexpected events.

Rowing Comparison:

Life jackets, coaching launches, and safety protocols. You do not row without protection when risk increases.

Liquidity

Financial Definition:

How easily money can be accessed without penalty or delay.

Rowing Comparison:

Ability to adjust rate or pressure mid-race. Flexibility creates options.

Net Worth

Financial Definition:

Assets minus liabilities.

Rowing Comparison:

Your final time. Not one stroke, but the full race outcome.

Rebalancing

Financial Definition:

Adjusting investments back to their intended mix over time.

Rowing Comparison:

Mid-race technical adjustments. Small corrections restore rhythm and balance.

Risk

Financial Definition:

The chance that outcomes differ from expectations, including loss.

Rowing Comparison:

Course selection and conditions. Higher reward comes with greater exposure.

Roth IRA

Financial Definition:

A retirement account where money grows tax-free if rules are followed.

Rowing Comparison:

Front-loading disciplined training so the final kilometers feel cleaner.

Stocks

Financial Definition:

Ownership shares in a company.

Rowing Comparison:

Power strokes. They drive speed but require balance and control.

Tax-Advantaged Accounts

Financial Definition:

Accounts that provide tax benefits, often with rules and restrictions.

Rowing Comparison:

Structured training programs. Rules exist to improve long-term results.

Volatility

Financial Definition:

Short-term ups and downs in market value.

Rowing Comparison:

Boat wobble. Normal movement that only becomes a problem if you panic.

Permanent Loss

Financial Definition:

Money that cannot recover due to poor decisions or panic.

Rowing Comparison:

Catching a crab because fundamentals were abandoned.

Total Return

Financial Definition:

Investment return from both price growth and income.

Rowing Comparison:

Overall race performance. Every segment matters, not just the sprint.

Value Investing

Financial Definition:

Investing in assets believed to be undervalued.

Rowing Comparison:

Clean, efficient rowing. Less flash, more control, consistent speed.

Yield

Financial Definition:

Income generated from an investment.

Rowing Comparison:

Steady splits. Not dramatic, but reliable over distance.

Final Note

This glossary reinforces one core principle:

Financial success, like success in **rowing**, comes from balance, discipline, timing, and repetition.

That philosophy runs through **Rowing Money 101** and beyond competition.

Disclaimers

Educational Purpose Only

This book is for educational purposes only.

The information provided in **Rowing Money 101** is intended to help readers understand general financial concepts using rowing-based analogies. It is not individualized financial, investment, tax, legal, or insurance advice.

Every financial situation is different. Your goals, income, family circumstances, risk tolerance, and time horizon are unique. What works well for one person or one crew may not be appropriate for another.

Not Financial, Investment, Tax, or Legal Advice

Nothing in this book should be interpreted as a recommendation to buy, sell, or hold any specific investment, financial product, or strategy.

This book does not replace advice from qualified professionals, including but not limited to:

- Financial advisors
- Accountants or tax professionals
- Attorneys
- Insurance professionals

Before making financial decisions, readers should consult professionals who can evaluate their individual situation.

No Guarantees or Promises of Results

All investing involves risk, including the possible loss of principal.

Past performance does not guarantee future results. Markets fluctuate. Economic conditions change. Outcomes cannot be predicted or guaranteed.

The examples and scenarios in this book are illustrative only. They are designed to explain concepts and may not reflect actual results or real-world outcomes.

Tax and Legal Information

Any discussion of taxes, retirement accounts, estate planning, or legal structures in this book is general in nature.

Tax laws and regulations change frequently and vary by jurisdiction. Legal requirements differ based on location and personal circumstances. Readers should seek personalized tax or legal advice before acting on any information related to these topics.

Athlete and Career Considerations

This book discusses financial topics as they relate to athletes and former athletes, including career transitions, income changes, and life after competition.

It does not provide career placement services, employment advice, or guarantees related to income, compensation, or career success.

Use of Analogies

Rowing and sports analogies are used throughout this book to make financial concepts easier to understand.

These analogies are educational tools only and should not be interpreted literally. Financial decisions require analysis beyond analogy, including personal circumstances, risk tolerance, and professional guidance.

Personal Responsibility

By reading this book, you acknowledge that:

- You are responsible for your own financial decisions
- You understand that financial outcomes involve uncertainty
- You agree to seek appropriate professional guidance when needed

Education improves decision-making, but responsibility remains with the individual.

Contact Information

If you would like to learn more about the concepts discussed in this book or explore additional educational resources, Pat Brown can be found through public platforms including LinkedIn, Twitter, and standard Google search.

For questions specifically related to **Rowing Money 101**, Pat Brown can be contacted at:

info@rowingmoney101.com

Final Reminder

Financial success is built over time through discipline, planning, and consistency.

This book provides a framework, not a guarantee.

Use it as a guide, not a substitute for professional advice.

Pat Brown OLB, University of Kansas

Made in the USA
Monee, IL
04 November 2026

67387577R00148